THE KEY IS IN THE CLOSET

Prayer Strategies That Advance God's Kingdom

by

James Lilley

THE KEY IS IN THE CLOSET

PRAYER STRATEGIES THAT ADVANCE GOD'S KINGDOM

by James Lilley

Published by Nehemiah Books.

Printed in the United States of America.

ISBN: 978-0615675558

Author photo by Derek Wilson.
Cover and book design by Rob Mandino/Connect.

Table of Contents

Acknowledgements

I would like to thank Brian Doherty, Elaine Zani, Rev. Jonathan and Rev. Verna Del Turco, John Fay, Rev. Wayne and the late Karen Shirk, Rev. Tim and Jackie Schmidt, Rev. David and Kelly Case, Rev. Terry and Karen Yancey, Pastor Bob and Jane Wise, Rev. Rex and Kay Henry, my father, Harry Lilley, my late mother, Bonny Lilley, and my stepmother, Carol Lilley – all of whom co-labored with God to lay the foundation of Heaven in my heart. To Pastor Marios Ellinas and Rob Mandino, thanks for turning my vision into a reality and pushing me to finish this book: truly iron sharpens iron. To my wife and best friend, Verna, who has supported and believed in me during our 19-year journey together: I love you and look forward to the rest of our lives together. Most importantly, I am eternally grateful for Jesus Christ my Kinsman Redeemer.

Foreword

Nothing I could possibly commit to the space allotted for this Foreword will adequately express the deep respect and admiration I have in my heart for Pastor James Lilley, his household and this book.

I consider Pastors James and Verna among my greatest heroes of the faith. Their extraordinary family and ministry continually model a wholehearted commitment to Christ, outstanding leadership and exceptional character. Any teaching and equipping material coming forth from Pastor James is automatically a vehicle of personal and corporate transformation – especially a book on prayer.

For Pastor James, his home, and the Kingdom warriors he leads, prayer is not merely a well-functioning program among many other church initiatives; nor is it just a daily practice or discipline. Prayer is Pastor James' life: everything he is and does stems from and revolves around intimacy with God through prayer.

I joyfully celebrate the release of *The Key is in the Closet,* for it is a timely, rich and eagerly anticipated work in the body of Christ. This book is filled with riveting personal testimonies, exceptional biblical teaching, proven strategies for personal and corporate intercessory prayer, and Pastor James' unparalleled encouragement and edification from beginning to end. Moreover, as we read this book we have the opportunity to receive impartation from a man who dwells in and operates from "the secret place of the Most High."

I honor Pastor James as a most remarkable son of the

Living God, an excellent husband and father, a great leader, and a twenty-first century reformer – a revivalist who knows God and His ways and who co-labors with the Holy Spirit to facilitate an ever-widening revival in New England.

I thank Pastor James for writing the book and for inspiring us through his life and service to pursue God's world-changing, prayer-wrought breakthroughs.

May the resurrection power of Jesus Christ be released as we learn to access the key that's in the closet!

Glory to glory!

Marios Ellinas
Pastor, Author

Preface

When God called my wife Verna and I to pastor a small church in urban Waterbury, Connecticut, on April 26th, 1998, He called us into a battleground.

The church building, a worn and tired former banquet hall, had at last been put on the block by our district office. The hulking "for sale" sign staked out front seemed to taunt my mandate there. The roof leaked, the carpet reeked, the back of the church had become a dump for tires, ratty sofas and trash.

Bills were held on my secretary Angie's desk, piling up until enough money came in to pay for one or two of them at a time. The pile never seemed to get any smaller.

You see, after a previous moral failure at the church the devil had been able to come in and grab authority where he never should have. He wanted to take out the destiny this church would prove to have.

But God is always faithful and knew just what He wanted done at this forlorn but special place.

The first thing Verna and I did to take back God's ground was rip out that "for sale" sign and shout into the atmosphere, "This is where we are planted! We shall not be moved!" Then we called a special Sunday evening service, inviting back an associate pastor who had left on unpleasant terms. I surprised everybody with a foot washing service. Something broke as I washed and dried that pastor's feet. God opposes the proud but gives grace to the humble: as we humbled ourselves God came back into First Assembly in a glorious way! The devil no longer had that place to gain a stronghold, a foothold or even a toehold.

I wrote this book with the local pastor and church in mind. I have seen my pastor friends grow frustrated, side-tracked and burned-out. Churches like theirs have had a lack of systematic prayer. An alarming 1800 pastors are leaving the ministry every month. That is why I wrote this book: to destroy the works of the devil and put up hedges of protection around every ministry I can.

Books are containers of ideas. Drink from this one and be refreshed, renewed and changed.

As you read I pray you will let the principles flow like honey into your heart. These biblical truths continue to revolutionize our church and community. God wants to do the same thing for you, right where you are – all you have to do is believe!

Blessings on you,

Pastor James Lilley

1

My Prayer Journey

And these things we write to you that your joy may be full.

1 John 1:4

Since 1989, when I surrendered my life to Jesus Christ, I have been on a prayer journey. I have been learning how to commune with my Heavenly Father.

I grew up one of five children in a Catholic home, in a Catholic neighborhood, in a blue collar town outside of Boston, Massachusetts. My dad, Harry Lilley, was from Wakefield, near Boston, while Bonny Brown, my mom, hailed from "Chicago Land."

When I was three the family relocated to Chicago and Wisconsin and remained there until my mother's untimely death when I was eight years old. My dad packed up his kids and drove his big, old yellow Ford LTD back to Massachusetts. I remember the muffler dropping off somewhere on that trip and Dad pulling over and tying it up so we could continue. I love and respect my father and we enjoy a great relationship today.

The earliest memories I have of church life were of memorizing the "Our Father" and praying that prayer before I went to bed every night. When I was a little boy, just seven years old, I dutifully took my first communion classes and made the sacraments. My parents saw to this – it was what we all were expected to do. For this steady upbringing I thank my mom and my dad.

Looking back now I see that I always had a yearning to know God. I know that in my simple, innocent way I had connected with "my Father who art in Heaven"while at the same time sensing there was much more to know, something deep and mysterious to explore.

What I was longing for from that young age, even though I could not have put it into words then, was the kind of fellowship with Jesus Christ the apostle speaks of so powerfully in 1 John 1:3-7.

The key to the treasures of Heaven is an abundance of time with *"Our Father Which art in the prayer closet."*

It was a week after my eighth birthday when my mother died. It was sudden and we were all blindsided. I was lost, even with a great father who did all he could to carry on with the things of life.

It didn't take long before I made the decision to hang around with the wrong crowd. When I was just twelve years old I started getting into mischief, and quickly mischief turned to trouble. I was caught shoplifting. I was arrested as a teenager for having alcohol in my car. My brothers and I threw lots of keg parties at our house when Dad was at work. Once we were even brazen enough to have a party at our boss's home while we were supposed to be house sitting for him. It did not go well when he returned home and got into a fist fight with one of our drunken pals in his own driveway.

I was an accomplished sinner. It was when I turned my heart over to Jesus Christ on January 7th, 1989, under

Pastor Jonathan Del Turco's anointed preaching, that the ship of my life began to turn away from the rocks. Two weeks before that, Elaine Zani, the mother of friends of mine, had cared enough about me to interrupt me at work and talk with me about the love of Jesus. We talked about making a new start. In her obedience to the Spirit, an imperishable seed was planted.

I was taught, I began to understand *and I began to witness* that the key to communion with the Lord is in the closet. The key to the treasures of Heaven is an abundance of time with "our Father Which art in the prayer closet."

Jesus, in Matthew 6:6, couldn't make it any clearer:

> *But when you pray go into your closet*
> *and when you have shut the door, pray*
> *to your Father who is in the secret place,*
> *and your Father who sees in secret will*
> *reward you openly.*

Your Abba Daddy is patiently waiting for you in the secret place. He's waiting – waiting to fill you with all of His glory and healing. He's waiting to reveal divine strategies for your life. He's waiting to nurture the gift of faith. Faith, "the substance of things hoped for" (Hebrews 11:1), will flood your heart to overflowing in the closet. The substance of Heaven will pour into your spirit as you secret yourself away and just wait on Him (Isaiah 40:31).

From a very young age I was a wild child. But from eternity God is rich in mercy (Ephesians 2:4). He loved me, and He came and rescued me from my sinful self.

Now I'm praising my Savior, my Refuge and Redeemer, and taking and breaking the devil's kingdom every day of my life.

After I surrendered my heart to Jesus as a young man I started attending prayer meetings at Elaine Zani's home. She was about the age my mother would have been, and she was a friend even though I thought she was "one of those Jesus freaks." In Spirit-filled fellowship, and especially in prayer, God began separating me from my old ways and associations. Acts 2:42 and 2 Corinthians 13:14 tell of an intense desire to fellowship with the Holy Spirit and with other believers – that was the craving of my spirit.

In April of 1989 I joined Alpha Youth under the anointed, loving leadership of Pastor Wayne Shirk and his wife, Karen. So young in the faith, I would watch and soak up the way they prayed every Friday night. Through Bible studies the Word of God starting taking root. I soaked it all in and I took it to heart. I plunged in because I could see that this prayer time was doing good things in me and in those around me.

As a group we would use the power of prayer to release heavenly changes. We would cry out to God for personal revival. We would plead with God to change the lives of our friends, the young people of Revere, Massachusetts, my birthplace. "Show me Your Glory!" was one of our battle cries as we gathered in the streets of the city. Some nights we would pile into cars and go straight from prayer, filled with the anointing, to witness to the hookers and "johns" of Boston's notorious Combat Zone. It was prayer-powered battle training.

When I was 19, God plucked me from busy New England and deposited me halfway across the country at Central Christian College in McPherson, Kansas, smack dab in the middle of farm country. Talk about a shock to the system: the church I attended was literally surrounded by immense fields of wheat.

But I fell in love with the place and the people and the college. In the dormitories on many nights we would pore over the Bible, studying it and gleaning from it, and we'd pray together late into the night. College for me was a wonderful, four-year spiritual experience!

God patiently peeled away the hard covering of my heart, restoring me to the image of Himself that He always intended.

In Bible college I went deeper in prayer under the pastoral mentoring of Rev. David Case. Six years of his teaching and modeling marked my spiritual life deeply. In one of Pastor Case's "Live Free" retreats I received healing prayer: God, in His awesome loving-kindness, healed me of the wounds that were the result of the intense grief of losing my mother as a child.

God then took me into the wilderness with Him. Not a wilderness exactly, but close to it for a guy from Boston. From the window in my new office in Pastor Case's church where I was serving as a youth pastor, all I could see were fields of corn and wheat. Kansas was beautiful for sure, but I wasn't in Boston anymore.

I would meet Pastor Case for "early morning prayer"

in a little room with the county's smallest electric heater and we'd huddle around that thing to stay warm in the winter months, crying out to God and waiting for His wonderful presence.

We students would have many prayer meetings around the dorm and campus. My heart had finally found a home! It was in those precious times of prayer in Kansas, with my new brothers and sisters and by myself, that God patiently peeled away the hard covering of my heart, like the layers of an onion, restoring me to the image of Himself that He always intended (Genesis 1:26).

You could say I owe a lot to Kansas because that's where I met my best friend, Verna Peterson. Verna just captured my heart as I got to know her in 1990. After fasting and praying for a grand total of a day, I knew that I knew God meant Verna to be my wife. This Adam had finally found his missing rib, and after a joy-filled wedding at First Assembly of God in Rapid City, South Dakota, Verna, Jesus and I embarked on our journey together. That was August 7, 1993.

I can remember like it was yesterday the blue-black Kansas nights, sitting under shimmering stars and just pondering the promises of God the way Abraham must have. After a very successful youth ministry and a loving mentoring relationship (that continues today) with Pastor Case and his wife Kelly, I sensed it was coming time to move to where God would show us.

After seasons on the city streets of Massachusetts and the fruited plains of Kansas, God thought it was time for me to take my new bride to the circus. We joined up with Reithoffer Shows, America's third largest traveling amusements company. The owners of the carnival were believers, and they wanted their performers and hands to be ministered to. They were looking for a young couple to lead worship and help teach in their Christian school so we hit the road with the show.

I should tell you that the first thing Verna had me do, insisted I do really, was yank the burnt orange shag carpet out of our fifth-hand motor home and replace it with a lovely white berber carpet. She was putting her special touch to it to make it a home for us.

Verna and I were school teachers and assistant pastors with Reverend Rex and Kay Henry. We taught 21 students the word of God. In our Thursday Midnight Bible Study we taught and prayed with fire eaters, tightrope walkers, animal trainers, truck drivers, ride runners and tent riggers. We held church services on Thursdays at midnight and Sundays around the show's schedule and witnessed to the workers. It was in this colorful, hectic, migrant, often wild setting that God was teaching us more truths about faith, sowing and reaping, and about warfare prayer.

There were many times when we warred in the Spirit but one in particular stands out. I can see it so clearly even today. It was a day between shows when the rock music got loud, the workers were quarreling, close to swinging at each other, and even the management was in turmoil. It was overwhelming in the natural for this pair of young pastors. So we drove off-site with Rex's "dually" white Ford F350 diesel to a quiet park, and we let the devil have it. We took our God-given righteous authority in Jesus' name over every single demonic thing that was happening back at the circus. We have that right as a child of God. Luke 10:19 tells us that "all the power over the enemy" has been given unto us! Do we truly "get" that? Jesus says ALL the power over the enemy. Give God a shout of praise!

After that time of prayer, such a deep peace came upon Verna and me. "Great peace have they which love Thy law and nothing shall offend them," says Psalm 119: 165. At the carnival I learned that warfare is "joyfare."

After about nine months growing in faith in the carnival we made our way back to Kansas to put our home on the market, then headed east to Massachusetts, to Wakefield, just north of Boston. It was in Wakefield where we would start our evangelistic ministry. Verna and I preached God's word and once again lived by faith. For nearly two years we would routinely do forced fasts because, like our Kansas days, we didn't have much in the cupboard (though for sure we had each other and Jesus). In Wakefield God taught us new things about persevering prayer.

We united with Pastor Tim Schmidt and his wife, Jackie. He was pastoring Calvary Christian Church in Lynnfield, Massachusetts, a town near Wakefield. We sensed we needed to submit to his leadership to learn and strengthen. He was a growing pastor with a growing church. Pastor Tim poured into us like a father would. He and I would meet with a group of men on Wednesdays for early morning prayer and cry out to God.

I saw in the example of his faithful, steady prayer life how Pastor Tim was given the power to impact many lives through preaching, teaching and mentoring.

In this season of our lives Verna and I would leave our base in Lynnfield and travel and preach anywhere a door would open. We preached in New Hampshire, Massachusetts, Rhode Island and Connecticut.

The return to Wakefield, the preaching across New England, the discipleship under Pastor Tim – it was all part of a mandate I received while praying with Verna under the stars in Kansas on a summer evening back in 1993. I felt God whisper direction into my spirit. His words sounded like this: "I'm calling you back to New England to be a part of a great revival that will sweep all of New England."

In April of 1998, while preaching at a meeting in Waterbury, Connecticut – a tired, industrial city that had been called the "brass capital of the world" – the Spirit spoke to me. It was a witness to my spirit that said, "I want you to knock on the door of this church." "This church" happened to be a former banquet hall, now the First Assembly of God where today I am the Senior Pastor. I replied to God, "Father, if this is You, please speak the same thing to Verna." Like Gideon, I gave God a fleece. That evening, resting in the Marriott Hotel, Verna sat up in bed and spoke almost the same words: "I think we are supposed to knock on this door."

Through prayer and confirmation we took our first senior pastorate on April 26th, 1998, and all these years later our faithful God continues to move in increasingly powerful ways, from glory to glory. Why? I believe it is precisely because 2 Chronicles 7:14 is being fulfilled:

> *If My people who are called by My name*
> *will humble themselves, and pray and seek*

> *My face, and turn from their wicked ways, then I will hear from heaven, and will forgive their sin and heal their land.*

When we came here people were calling Waterbury the "sin city" of Connecticut. They even opened a nightclub with that same name. But I taught our leaders to speak blessings over the city as Proverbs 11:11 instructs: "By the blessing of the upright the city is exalted."

In unity we set a new focus. We claimed the godly heritage of the saints who, in the 1950s, built Holy Land USA on a prominent peak overlooking the heart of Waterbury and Interstate 84 as it cuts through the city, crowning it with a 25-foot-high illuminated cross. We began to declare Waterbury "Holy Land USA" and "the city of our God," and we are seeing the Holy Spirit visit this dear city in tangible ways.

It is at our church that I have learned how to apply the principles of overcoming prayer I share with you here. Take heart, have faith and enjoy this book. Enjoy your prayer journey and you will learn to love the closet!

2

The Place and Structure of Prayer

Now in the morning, having risen a long while before daylight,
He went out and departed to a solitary place; and there he prayed.

MARK 1:35

In your place of prayer you will find keys to:

1. Communion with God (Zechariah 4:1-6);
2. City-taking strategies (1 Corinthians 2:9-10); and
3. Crisis cures (2 Chronicles 20, 2 Samuel 5).

The early chapters of Zechariah are enlightening. In Zechariah 3:4 God calls us into the righteousness of Christ – He has exchanged our filthy rags of sin for His pure, rich robes. Zechariah 4, with its prophetic gold lampstand and two olive trees, is a great passage of Scripture. The Lord calls us to be Spirit-empowered (Zechariah 4:6) and to move mountains (Zechariah 4:7) but only after we have been filled with His righteousness and His presence.

I've found that the best place to receive impartations from the presence of the Holy Spirit is in the place of prayer. By this I don't mean a literal, physical place (I'll speak about that later on), I mean the spiritual place of prayer, wherever I am.

Most of the great revelations and insights God has given me were in my prayer closet (again, not a single place). Lots of times God wakes me up in the middle of the night and talks to me (Zechariah 4:1), fellowshipping with me and showing me what He wants me to do in the days ahead.

In September of 2000 God gave me this word at a leadership prayer meeting: "This ministry will rise or fall according to its level of prayer." Wow – that crystal clear word from God has proven itself to be life changing and ministry impacting. I believe it is a word for you, too.

God gave me this word... ***"This ministry will rise or fall according to its level of prayer."***

From that day forward I made prayer the number one focus of my life. I put an end to my old mindset that, despite craving time with the Lord and witnessing mountains move by the power of prayer, would nonetheless say, "Later, Lord, please, when I get around to praying. I can't get out of bed and visit with you now," (like the Shulamite woman in Song of Solomon 5:3). Today, prayer is my lifeline. It's the place where I'm changed. It's the pivot point upon which my life and ministry will rise or fall.

With that unmistakable statement from God fresh in our hearts, our church leadership and I started corporate prayer on Friday nights. We had wonderful times of prayer coupled with praise and worship. Some nights we would war in the Spirit. Some nights were more meditative and we would just wait in the presence of our King. Other nights joy would break out. Whatever the atmosphere, it was in the "place of prayer" that God's Spirit would impart what I needed, and what our church needed, at that time.

Friends, I have to tell you that something restricting and oppressive over our church was broken in the Spirit in 2000 because of these praise and prayer evenings. As in Luke 3:21, now we are blessed with an open heaven:

> *When all the people were baptized, it came to pass that Jesus also was baptized; and while He prayed, the heaven was opened.*

That same year I went on a personal prayer and fasting retreat to Los Angeles, to Prayer Mountain, founded by Mama Choi. Mama Choi was the creator of the trans-denominational organization of Christian women called Aglow International and one of the birthing prayer warriors of the world's largest church, the Yoido Full Gospel Church in Seoul, South Korea. She was also the mother-in-law of Dr. David Yonggi Cho who pastors Yoido Full Gospel. She used her God-given authority (Luke 10:19) to supernaturally defeat demonic-inspired witches and warlocks. God gave her 40 acres in the suburbs of Los Angeles to be a refuge where prayer and fasting retreats could take place.

While fasting, praying and waiting on the Lord at Prayer Mountain God spoke to me. His message added to those original words He gave me about the absolute necessity of prayer for overcoming: "Every thing you need in your life, family and church must be birthed by fervent prayer, words of faith and acts of courage."

It was at this time I began making faith-filled prayer lists, writing them down on paper and birthing them into the natural realm by fervent prayer and words of faith. We must give birth to our desires from God (John 15:6,7 and Psalm 37:4). Faith is the substance of things hoped for and the evidence of things not seen, the Bible teaches us, and without it you can't please God (Hebrews 11:1, 6). It's the substance of heaven and the spiritual realm. It's what the Holy Spirit fills your heart with as you seek Him. It's pregnant with all the things you will ever need on this earth. And prayer is the language of faith.

God spoke again...
"Everything you need in your life, family and church must be birthed by fervent prayer, words of faith and acts of courage."

God knows the things you need! Even when you do not, He does. In His presence – in prayer, in the secret place – is fullness of joy and pleasures evermore (Psalm 16:11). When you get into His presence and when you enjoy enjoy reading His word, the substance of Heaven fills your spirit-man. The Lord fills you with things hoped for and things not seen.

Everything you will ever need – every key to an overcoming life – is found in His manifest presence. That is why it is so critical for you to make it a habit to go to your place of prayer every morning.

Jesus said to Peter, "And I will give you the keys of

the kingdom of heaven" (Matthew 16:19). Not a key, but the keys. Jesus has many keys to release to you in your prayer closet.

The Structure of Prayer, Jesus' Way

Order comes first, then glory. Let's follow the lead of Jesus as we develop our own orderly habits of prayer. Let's see what the Master did. In Mark 1:35 we read:

> *Now in the morning, having risen a long while before daylight, He went out and departed to a solitary place; and there He prayed.*

This little passage shows us that Jesus had a set time, a set place and a set plan. It's so simple and so essential. It probably seems so obvious to you, but with any of these fundamentals to successful prayer absent we might flounder. Can you relate?

Incorporating new structure and fresh commitment into your prayer life will enable you to flow from discipline to desire to delight!

Set a time. Jesus did it! Set your mind like flint for the next 30 days: "I will get up every morning at 6 A.M. and pray and seek God's face." You set a time that works for your life, though I suggest the morning "before the world rushes in again," to quote a lyric by Newsong on this same subject. Whatever the time, stick to it. Don't permit the demands of this world to crowd out your divine appointment.

You will find that the more successful you become in your ministry and your life the more you must guard your prayer and study time. The world, your old ways and your enemy will relentlessly try to pull you away from it, but great leaders know how to spend time in quiet and solitude!

Set a place. You really need to find a quiet place where you will consistently have your quiet time. You must. I have a chair and table I go to in the morning, before the house gets going, to pray, read the word, worship my Abba and journal. You must have a place to go to worship alone, *solitario*, by yourself, in solitude, with nobody around! The Bible refers to it as a "secret place." For me it began outside next to a wheat field in Kansas; in the traveling carnival it was in our RV; in Wakefield it was in the woods; in Waterbury it was out behind my house near a brook on a rock. Today, it is in my desk chair, or in my cottage on the shore of the pond.

We need to shut away the sounds of the world so that we may hear the voice of God.

We need to shut away the sounds of the world so that we may hear the voice of God. Set a place to experience fellowship with the Holy Spirit (2 Corinthians 13:14) and get ready: He will fill you with the substance of Heaven.

Set a plan. It really does help to set a plan by which you will springboard into God's presence. What will you read when you come into your secret place? I always read a portion of the word of God and ask the Holy Spirit to give me revelation to live by (Ephesians 1:17,18). I want to be a man of divine purpose, divine plans and divine presence (Exodus 33:13-18). God's gracious presence is the one thing that separates us from the world as God's people. The presence and grace of the Holy Spirit is so precious to us as believers – without them we as a church are not much more than just another civic club.

What's your plan going to be? How much Scripture will you read? What book of the Bible will you study? I suggest you pick one and become an expert at that book. Study the word to become a capable workman:

> *Be diligent to present yourself approved to God, a worker who does not need to be ashamed, rightly dividing the word of truth.*
>
> 2 Timothy 2:15

Don't act like a Pharisee. Because much of your life is driven by calendars, clocks, appointments, schedules and the demands and needs of others, the spontaneous days off are some of the sweetest days. The same reality applies to your prayer time. Absolutely spend time in structure to keep your flesh disciplined, but when the Holy Spirit shows up in force enjoy some spontaneity! Take your thoughts captive (2 Corinthians 10:5) and don't get even a little bit rigid and pharisaical.

Flow with the Holy Spirit. "Spirit and structure" is the word of the hour – you need both, my friend! That is how you build a great life, a great family and a great church. All Spirit and you will blow up. All structure and you will dry up. Have both and you will go up.

As I close this chapter let me share a Scripture and a brief story with you.

You'll recall these words from 1 Corinthians 2:8,9:

> *But as it is written: "Eye has not seen, nor ear heard, nor have entered into the heart of man the things which God has prepared for those who love Him." But God has revealed them to us through His Spirit. For the Spirit searches all things, yes, the deep things of God.*

Oh, hear my heart. The place of prayer is the place of impartation and revelation. It is the place of strategies and crisis cures.

I was on my face praying to my Father while in my first office at First Assembly of God when He "dropped" the two houses and parking lots that are next door to our church into my spirit. I saw those two houses come into my spirit. I knew that I knew they belonged to the Kingdom of God! As if that weren't enough the Lord witnessed to me, "Those two houses are yours." I couldn't miss it. God had impregnated me with the faith I would need. I remember praising God, pulling myself up off that old blue carpet knowing that God had clearly imparted special, sustaining revelation into my spirit as He and I had been communing. God's revelation was bringing lifestyle transformation.

But let me tell you it didn't just all ease into place! No, that would be the beginning of a drawn-out prayer battle in the Spirit to take back those houses from the dope filled, beer drenched, devil filled dives they had become and put them to the uses God had planned all along. It was a battle in the heavenlies and God showed up like we knew He would. At the end of two years we were more than conquerors through the Spirit. (More on this in Chapter Three.)

Oh, hear my heart: the place of prayer is the place of impartation and revelation. It is the place of strategies and crisis cures. You will never advance the Kingdom of God on earth apart from the "place of prayer."

May we all be found in that place daily because truly the key to overcoming the world is in the closet. Let us never forget God's words in Zechariah 4:6 – " 'Not by might nor by power, but by my Spirit,' says the Lord of hosts."

3

Prayer and Faith

For we walk by faith, not by sight.

2 Corinthians 5:7

I will stand my watch and set myself on the rampart, and watch to see what He will say to me, and what I will answer when I am corrected. Then the LORD answered me and said: "Write the vision and make it plain on tablets that he may run when he reads it. For the vision is yet for an appointed time; But at the end it will speak, and it will not lie. Though it tarries, wait for it; because it will surely come, it will not tarry. Behold the proud, his soul is not upright in him; but the just shall live by his faith.

Habakkuk 2:1-4

The prophet Habakkuk had troubling questions about the violence taking place all about him. Sin was flourishing in the city of Jerusalem – contention, cruelty, plundering, strife. Evil was consuming the capital of the Jewish people and the man of God was overwhelmed by it. He did not see God's word penetrating the evil that was saturating the place.

What was Habakkuk's response? In faith he settled into his prayer closet. He took to the ramparts in prayer. He went to the wall where watchmen scan their territory for enemies who would come and plunder the city.

Like Habakkuk, you and I are meant to be faithful watchmen on our own walls.

The prophet Isaiah speaks God's timeless word, echoing Habakkuk on being vigilant:

> *I have posted watchmen on your walls,*
> *O Jerusalem; they will never be silent*
> *day or night.*
>
> ISAIAH 62:6

In Matthew 26:41 Jesus also exhorts us to "watch and pray, lest you enter into temptation."

During those times in our lives when the troubling situations seem to keep coming at us one after another, we are not to flee. We are to set ourselves up on our ramparts and wait on the Lord, keeping "watch" for Him. We are called to be sober and vigilant and to overcome the devil thru steadfast faith in our victorious Father:

> *Be sober, be vigilant; because your adversary*
> *the devil walks about like a roaring lion,*
> *seeking whom he may devour. Resist him,*
> *steadfast in the faith, knowing that the same*
> *sufferings are experienced by your brother-*
> *hood in the world.*
>
> 1 PETER 5:8,9

Habakkuk received the answers to his questioning prayers. What did the Lord tell him to do? Let's read again from Habakkuk 2:2,3:

> *Write the vision, and make it plain on the tablets that he may run who reads it. For the vision is yet for an appointed time. But at the end it will speak, and it will not lie. Though it tarries, wait for it, because it will surely come, it will not tarry.*

In Genesis 12, God gave to Abraham a vision of a promised Son who would bless the world. That vision did not come to pass until 25 years later (Genesis 21). Although God gives you a vision it could "tarry" months, years or even decades before the complete vision has come to pass. What I'm trying to say is that you must trust and understand the role God's timing plays in your vision.

Like Habakkuk, you and I are meant to be faithful watchmen on our own walls.

There is *chronos* time and *kairos* time in the Bible. *Chronos* is the way we keep track of the hours and minutes in a day on planet earth. It is quantitative. Yet when God steps into our particular time and place we call it *kairos* time – a special time, the right time at which something supernatural happens.

As I mature as a believer I am learning how to better discern God's precious *kairos* time. In Genesis 8:22 there is seed time, then a harvest. We need to discern the "time part" of that verse and just how it applies to our lives.

Prayer is the place of vision! It's the place where Almighty God speaks His vision and faith into your human spirit. I do not believe that we can truly grasp the greatness of that privilege.

Day-In, Day-Out Relentless Faith

Habakkuk 2:4 tells us the way we are meant to live: *"...the just shall live by his faith."* As Paul writes in the first chapter of Ephesians, living in faith is the place where the eyes of your understanding are opened to see your calling, your inheritance and the great power of God that flows through the people who believe.

Have you ever felt drained and ready to surrender? I have. Many times. We all have. But each time I have chosen to respond by going into my prayer closet to wait on my rescuer Jesus, to worship Him, to sing to Him, to read His words. Each time my spirit has never failed to revive and mount up with eagle's wings. I have always been made ready to walk and run again (Isaiah 40:31).

It is clear: we must be people of relentless faith. We must allow the faith of God to fill us up every day. *Every day*. Because we know from Romans 10:17 that faith comes by hearing and hearing by the word of God, you absolutely must keep hearing, hearing, hearing and hearing God's word. Man lives – truly lives, overcomes, fulfills his God-ordained destiny, reaches the lost of the world – by every word that proceeds from the mouth of the Lord (Deuteronomy 8:3).

As you arrive at each higher level in your walk with Jesus you must receive fresh directions from your Father.

Here's a simple little suggestion that has helped me and my family literally hear God's direction. Get a recorded edition of the Bible. Play the recorded word of God in your car. Use your iPod or Blackberry and bathe in the word on a walk, at your desk, cooking dinner, mowing the lawn. Even better, let God's word flow through the atmosphere of your home with your kids around. Decide to allow your Father's word to replace the other "noises" that creep into our lives. Let the word ring out when you're in the shower. Play it softly as you fall to sleep at night – and get ready to be filled with what Hebrews 11:1 calls "now faith." (I believe "now" as it is used here is not so much a simple word joining the writer's sentences as it is an adjective that describes an "immediate" kind of faith!)

It's in your prayer closet that "immediate faith" recharges you and equips you. Hebrews 11:1 teaches us:

> *Now faith is the substance of things hoped for,*
> *the evidence of things not seen.*

Faith is a real substance that first fills your Spirit and then manifests itself upon the earth as you pray, listen and declare.

Let's dig some more from Hebrews 11:1. Let's mine it for gold nuggets from God. This is my favorite chapter in the Bible. This chapter shows us how to live what William Carey, the father of modern missions, loved to preach:

1. Believe great things from God
2. Attempt great things for God.

I see Hebrews 11 teaching is how to do that by faith. Hebrews 11:1 instructs us that faith is the substance of the things we hope for and the evidence of things we do not see with our eyes.

Faith is a Substance

We get the word "substance" here from the Greek word "*hupostasis,*" which means, "that which has a firm foundation upon which things are built." The inspired author of Hebrews also knew "*hupostasis*" as a term used in the legal profession where it meant, "to overcome; under authority [of God's word and kingdom] as well as to hold the title deed – complete, legal ownership – to something tangible. [*Taking land for God's kingdom – God is into real estate!*]" That is the tangible reality of the invisible faith of those who believe.

My dictionary tells me that "substance" is "the actual matter of a thing." Faith is a substance from the spiritual realm. When you arrive under God's authority He will download instructions into your spirit that will manifest in the earth by faith (but it must be in God's timing). Spirit-to-spirit communication is the highest possible realm of communication we can experience.

Faith is Evidence

Faith is also the "evidence," the proof, of things not seen. Translated from the Greek word "*elegchos*" the writer invokes another image from man's legal system that we can understand. Evidence refers to the "thing" by which something is tested and proven and by which a verdict is reached. It implies a jury hearing the facts presented and being convinced by the testimonies. God is the righteous lawgiver and judge and King (Isaiah 33:22) and the spiritual picture here is that of a Heavenly courtroom where we as believers come before an awesome, righteous Judge and King to receive a ruling in our favor, thanks solely to the wonderful payment Jesus already made for us!

Seeing "Things" In the Spirit

This short verse says twice that faith is connected with things. I believe that "things" are the people, objects, situations and movements of the Spirit that God wishes to get to you so that His will for your life can be fulfilled, for all God's plans for us are good (Jeremiah 29:11). These things are only seen and received in the Spirit. Ephesians 1:3 says that God has blessed us with every blessing in the Spirit. These blessings must be "pulled down" from the spirit realm into the earth realm. God creates "things" in the spirit realm. This is the unseen, eternal realm that is more real than what we see with our physical eyes.

> **God creates "things" in the spirit realm. This is the unseen, eternal realm that is more real than what we see with our eyes.**

Your faith cannot create "things." Your Father does that; your faith stirred into action is made for obtaining things that already exist in the spirit realm. The word of God creates! There are thousands of promises in the

Spiritual realm for you. Warehouses of blessings are waiting for you to access them. Accessing these blessings fulfills destinies.

Hebrews 12:2 says that Jesus is the author and finisher or perfector of our faith. He knows what we need to begin our race and what we need to finish our race. The key element for God's people is to have a spirit of prayer and faith about them. The words "by faith" are a steady proclamation found 22 times in Chapter 11 of Hebrews. We must wait in His presence to be filled with "now faith" so we can go forward and execute our Savior's plans, by faith.

We read in Hebrews 11:2, "For by faith the elders obtained a good report" and that is how you, too, will please your Father and obtain a good report. Surely you have had some victories in the past, which is great. But like God told an elderly Joshua, there is much more land to take (Joshua 13:1). Your promised land is waiting for you to possess. Hit your prayer closet, be filled with the faith of God, and take back the ground that God meant for you to have!

Faith That Endures

In the previous chapter I told how, as I was crying out to my Father, the Spirit deposited the properties next door to our church right into my spirit. The clarity with which I saw the transaction from heaven was amazing. There was no doubt that the houses belonged to the Kingdom of God – but little did I know I would have a two-and-a-half year fight in prayer to win them. (This was a situation in which I really learned the Timing Principle.) I lived like the persistent widow in Jesus' parable (Luke 18:1-8), praying and not losing heart.

Faith is such a key for God's people. Faith is the only way we please God and faith is the only way we receive from God (Hebrews 11:6). It's the spiritual substance that sets God's people apart from the world. Without faith our churches are just social clubs. The just are to "live by faith" and to "walk by faith." This is our calling – so let's go for it!

It astounds me that in most American seminaries there are no faith classes. Jesus often asked his disciples, with a question that holds its own answer, "Why are you fearful, O you of little faith?" (Matthew 8:26). Jesus could do no mighty work in Nazareth. Why? Because of unbelief in that place (Mark 6:1-5). Jesus was always stirring up people's faith. We must decide to feed our faith and starve our doubts every day. Jesus was always speaking to the wind, to trees, to sick people, to demons – faith speaks God's word!

> **Hit your prayer closet, be filled with the faith of God, and take back the ground that was meant for you!**

Rhema and Persistence

In Mark 11:23 we read:

> *For assuredly, I say to you, whoever says to this mountain, 'Be removed and be cast into the sea,' and does not doubt in his heart, but*

> *believes that those things he says will be done, he will have whatever he says*

Speak to the mountains in your life by faith, friend – don't climb them!

Faith pulls down the promises of God into our spirit and then faith speaks. Faith has a voice (Romans 4:17). Focused thinking and faith speaking advances God's kingdom. Faith comes by hearing and hearing by the word of God (Romans 10:17) while fear comes by hearing and believing the report of man.

Focused thinking and faith speaking advances God's kingdom. Speak to the mountains in your life by faith – don't climb them!

There is a *logos* word and a *rhema* word from God. These are the two Greek nouns in the New Testament for "word." Psalm 119:89 says that the *logos* is forever settled in the heavens; this is the written word of God that we read. No part of it will ever change. But the *rhema* word is God's word spoken into your spirit. This is the still, small voice you hear when you read the Bible, the *rhema* word when reading the *logos* word.

Matthew 4:4 uses the word *rhema* when Jesus says, "Man shall not live by bread alone, but by every word [*rhema*] that proceeds from the mouth of God." This is the way man lives the abundant life in Christ.

Prayer is the place of vision and faith. Just last week I was faced with a ministry crossroad. I was double-minded. So I turned my plate over, went into my prayer closet and sought God's face for direction for my life and ministry. I'll tell you that God broke through with such clarity that now I'm running full steam ahead – praise His holy name!

Let's return to the prayer room and receive vision and faith revelation from God's Spirit. If we will do that we can run the race with faith and please God. Truly the key is in the closet.

Never forget that satan, the "old serpent," rolls out the same tired (but sadly effective) tricks again and again, and one of the most effective has to be his subtlety. He speaks very subtly to our spirit. He casts doubts. He desires to stick you in self-doubt – "Did God really say that? " – which leads to indecision. When you're stuck in double-minded indecision you are paralyzed and you don't go anywhere with the passion and zeal God had intended for you.

When you're stuck you need a word from God to get unstuck. Look at 1 Samuel 3:1:

> *Now the boy Samuel ministered to the LORD before Eli. And the word of the LORD was rare in those days; there was no widespread revelation.*

The Hebrew word for "widespread" is "*parats*" which translates into English as "break out or burst out." You must receive God's word for a breakout into your next season. The word of God will get you unstuck!

So speak into yourself, "I have a Joshua and Caleb spirit! I'm going into my promised land and no devil in hell is going to stop me. I am well able to overcome anything that comes my way!" Be like Caleb in Numbers 13:30 and don't imitate the complainers of Numbers 14 who received the rotten fruit of all their complaining. Complain and you will remain. Stop your complaining and start obtaining.

It took 14 years from the time God gave me His vision for a revival as I met with Him in the wheat fields of Kansas in 1993 to the partial fulfillment in New England in 2007. I saw another greater dimension when I traveled with a prayer and praise team to Boston in January of 2010. When the Holy Spirit ministered to that church, I sat amazed and blessed as the Counselor reminded me of His call on my life.

Worship while you wait! Build a throne of praise.

Paul encouraged the citizens of Thessalonica (1 Thessalonians 5:16-18) with these words:

> *Rejoice always, pray without ceasing, in everything give thanks; for this is the will of God in Christ Jesus for you.*

Worship while you wait! Build a throne of praise. As you persist in the closet in prayer and faith God will break through into your life and give you breakout. He is Jehovah-nissi, "The Lord Our Banner," our "Victory God" (Exodus 17:8-16).

Waiting time in the prayer closet is never wasted

time. It is precious time. In it God delivers "power from on high" (Luke 24:49). Get filled with faith and fulfill His calling on your life. Get filled with His faith and then run in the vision, for it will surely come to pass if you run in prayer, faith and patience. AMEN!

4

Prayer and the Promises of God

He is a rewarder of those who diligently seek Him.

Hebrews 11:6

Promises Reveal God's Desires for Us

Scholars say there are 8,610 promises from God to man in the Holy Scriptures. To get them into our spirits so that we not only *know* them but that we *operate* in their power, it is important that we read and meditate on God's holy word every day.

The Apostle Paul illuminated young Timothy:

> *All Scripture is given by inspiration of God, and is profitable for doctrine, for reproof, for correction, for instruction in righteousness....*
>
> 2 Timothy 3:16

And the first three verses of the very first psalm in the Bible tell us:

> *Blessed is the man who walks not in the counsel of the ungodly,*
> *Nor stands in the path of sinners,*
> *Nor sits in the seat of the scornful;*
> *But his delight is in the law of the LORD,*

And in His law he meditates day and night.
He shall be like a tree
Planted by the rivers of water,
That brings forth its fruit in its season,
Whose leaf also shall not wither;
And whatever he does shall prosper.

PSALM 1: 1-3

As we take the Scriptures into ourselves the old self peels away and we are gifted with our true identity, the one which God meant for us all along.

The Apostle Paul's prayers in Ephesians 1 ask God to open the eyes of that church's understanding to see life-changing, city-taking, spiritual truths about who they are *when they believe*. These truths apply every bit as much to believers all these centuries later. In faith *we* will also see the hope of our calling, the riches of the glory of our inheritance in the saints, the greatness of the power that works in us and through us, and the power of the completed work of Christ's death, burial and resurrection!

The devil just loves to "punch out" our identity. In Matthew 4 we see that was how he first challenged Jesus: "If you are the Son of God..." he said. If? ***IF?*** Does that sound like a taunt to you?

Jesus then delivered a "Spirit haymaker" punch to that old deceiver:

But He answered and said, "It is written, 'Man shall not live by bread alone, but by every word that proceeds from the mouth of God.'"

MATTHEW 4:4

Through the word for you from your Abba: that's how you will see your identity and how you will really live in the fullness of all His promises. We all need to get the revelation of God as our "Abba," our Daddy, our Papa God (Galatians 4:6).

Lately I've been walking around singing the words of Israel Houghton's song, "I Know Who I Am," as my personal declaration – have you heard them?

I know who I am,
I know who I am,
I know who I am
I am Yours, I am Yours.

I was broken and You healed me.
I was dying and You gave me life
Lord, You are my identity
*I know, I know.**

There are so many blessings God wants to bestow upon His children, especially the identity of being in Him, but He only reveals them *in richness* to those who diligently seek Him:

> *But without faith it is impossible to please Him, for he who comes to God must believe that He is, and that He is a rewarder of those who diligently seek Him.*
>
> Hebrews 11:6

* "I Know Who I Am," Israel Houghton, Chris Tomlin, "A Deeper Level," 2007, Integrity Music.

In Deuteronomy 6:11 our Father gives us awesome promises for provision that become ours as we believe, as we love Him with all of our heart, soul, mind, and strength:

- Large and beautiful cities which you did not build;
- Houses full of all good things;
- Wells of water which you did not dig; and
- Vineyards of fruit which you did not plant.

There are so many blessings God wants to bestow... but He only reveals them *in richness* to those who diligently seek Him.

Deuteronomy 6:12 adds a note of caution: "…then beware, lest you forget the Lord who brought you out of the land of Egypt, from the house of bondage."

So beat down pridefulness after you have your victories or experience some prosperity. They are a gift from God anyway. And you still have land to take, you still have more intimate places to go with your Father. Don't cash in, cast into deeper waters.

More Promises

What awesome promises God has for us, yes? Let's look at some more of the biggest:

- You are a son of Abraham, an heir according to the promise (Galatians 3:25-4:7);

waiting in your prayer closet. Like the gifts they are, promises will be unwrapped and opened for you if you will seek after Him (Psalm 63, Matthew 7:7). So let's go forward now and attain every promise God has for us!

5

Prayer and Prophetic Acts

Then he said to the king of Israel, "Put your hand on the bow." So he put his hand on it, and Elisha put his hands on the king's hands.

2 Kings 3:16

If I believe in prayer, and if I believe that God speaks to me in that place of prayer, then why would I not be obedient to any instruction my Father gives me in prayer? "If you love me you will obey me," Jesus says in John 14:15. Our obedience to the things God shows us shows God that we love Him!

I was listening to a sermon on cassette years ago by Paul Yonggi Cho, who pastors the world's largest church, the Yoido Full Gospel Church in South Korea. On that tape he was asked how his church had grown to over 800,000 members. He responded simply, "I just pray and obey. *Ha ha ha!*" His chuckle was as if to add, "*Of course!*" It boils down to that: being in intimate prayer relationship with your Father, and doing as He directs, will tune you in to His plans and purposes and empower you to be used mightily for the kingdom.

In both the Old and New Testaments we read time and time again of prophetic acts by an individual after hearing from God. Two come to my mind right away: Moses who listened to God at the bitter wells of Marah and threw a stick into the waters, foreshadowing the cross of Christ, to change them from deadly to life-giving (Exodus 15); and Philip responding to the Spirit's prompting, "Go near and overtake this chariot," so that the Ethiopian queen's eunuch, a man of great authority with control over her treasury, could receive and rejoice over the seed of new life in Jesus, a seed that yielded abundant fruit in his home country.

This is obedience to the Holy Spirit. Obedience is cooperation. It is the opposite of rebellion. It is the opposite of selfishness. Revelation 22:17 says, "...the Spirit and the bride say, 'Come!'..." The Spirit is directing the bride and the bride is in obedience to the Spirit.

When we are obedient to the Spirit we release the kingdom of God on earth.

When we are tuned in through prayer we're working and flowing together with our God in a joint partnership (wow!), even when we truly don't know what to pray for:

> *Likewise the Spirit also helps in our weaknesses. For we do not know what we should pray for as we ought, but the Spirit Himself makes intercession for us with groanings which cannot be uttered.*
>
> ROMANS 8:28

When we are obedient to the Spirit we release the kingdom of God on earth.

This applies to my times of leadership, even during our Sunday services. In the time leading up to the first service you could say that I'm "seeker sensitive," as I ought to be, but when the praise and worship begins I shift into "Spirit sensitive." I'm looking for the direction of the Holy Spirit. I'm waiting on it. I want to receive the revelation of the Spirit, then obey it and move in it.

That's what David did in 2 Samuel 5. The Philistines came against him after they heard he was anointed ruler over Israel – what a testing! David didn't turn inward and rely on his own military savvy, which was considerable, but instead cried out to God, *asking in prayer* whether he should go up against the Philistines who were all deployed and waiting. God said yes, He would "doubtless deliver them" into David's hand. David obeyed, and the Philistines were routed.

> **David didn't turn inward and rely on his own military savvy but instead cried out to God, *asking in prayer....***

But the testing came again when the scattered Philistine army regrouped, lumbered back, and dug into the same valley yet again waiting for the king. Did David figure, "We routed them once, we'll do it again?" If you know the story you know David clung to his Jehovah-nissi and received a precious bit of military counsel from God: circle around the enemy and attack from the back side after you hear the sound of marching in the tops of the mulberry trees. Then the Lord went ahead of David and did the "heavy lifting." This second time David pushed the Philistines all the way out. The moral of that story? Praying, trusting and obeying God's Spirit brought victory!

There is a powerful illustration in 2 Kings, a story with a very different outcome. It's a story about a king who disobeys the word of the King:

> *Elisha had become sick with the illness of which he would die. Then Joash the king of Israel came down to him, and wept over his face, and said, "O my father, my father, the chariots of Israel and their horsemen!" And Elisha said to him, "Take a bow and some arrows." So he took himself a bow and some arrows. Then he said to the king of Israel, "Put your hand on the bow." So he put his hand on it, and Elisha put his hands on the king's hands. And he said, "Open the east window;" and he opened it. Then Elisha said, "Shoot"; and he shot. And he said, "The arrow of the LORD's deliverance and the arrow of deliverance from Syria; for you must strike the Syrians at Aphek till you have destroyed them." Then he said, "Take the arrows;" so he took them. And he said to the king of Israel, "Strike the ground;" so he struck three times, and stopped. And the man of God was angry with him, and said, "You should have struck five or six times; then you would have struck Syria till you had destroyed it! But now you will strike Syria only three times." Then Elisha died,*

and they buried him. And the raiding bands from Moab invaded the land in the spring of the year.

2 KINGS 13:14-20

What a powerful section of Scripture. What a lesson for us. When Elisha told King Joash to take a bow and some arrows, when Elisha laid his hands on the king's hands and they shot the arrows out the east window together, the hands of the prophet of God became the king's hands; the prophet of God's vision became his vision.

When we do what He says we release the kingdom of God into this visible, flesh-and-blood earth realm.

Then Joash was told to strike the ground with the arrows in his hand. He did, three times. This frustrated and dismayed the man of God – these were arrows of the Lord's deliverance and arrows of deliverance from the Syrian enemy! Had he struck the ground five or six times he would have clobbered Syria mortally in the spirit and then seen their total destruction in the natural. Not striking a full measure translated into a shortcoming in obedience. God expected a warrior attitude and action to come forth out of the king. He did not expect the unsure, halfway or lukewarm. The King was displeased with the attitude of the king.

When we hear the still, gentle voice of the Holy Spirit and then do what He says we release the kingdom of God from the spiritual realm into this visible, flesh-and-blood earth realm. God works through obedient vessels but He will not advance information to you beyond your last act of disobedience.

Take this to heart: Joash's enemy not only remained, they actually advanced, raiding and invading Joash's land when the man of God died. In the same way, when the prophetic prayer spirit dies in your ministry the enemy will invade your territory.

Claiming Ground for Jehovah-Nissi Today

While in prayer one evening back in 2004 God spoke to my spirit. I heard Him say, "Go, shoot an arrow into the Waterville Lumber property." This was the vacant lot and empty buildings, a former lumber yard, located next door to our church property. God had already spoken to me that same year out of His word, from Joshua 1:3: "Every place that the sole of your foot will tread upon I have given you, as I said to Moses."

Did you know that "tread" can be translated as "bend the bow, go to war for?" That is a literal translation of the Hebrew. He is saying that every land you war for by faith I will give to you. That's a promise from the Lord of Hosts. If He's leading you to take property for His kingdom you must buy it with your prayers. You must war in the Spirit for it, firing verses like Psalm 125:3: "For the scepter of wickedness shall not rest on the land allotted to the righteous...."

I recruited Jason Stillwell and Elijah Mickelson, my younger associates at the time, to believe God with me about the lumber company property and to go with me to shoot an arrow into the side of one of the abandoned buildings. The bow and arrow I used I bought in Ghana, Africa, while on a missions trip a couple of years before for $3. (Though inexpensive it has become a priceless symbol to me. I keep the arrow in my office and look at it every day.) We left that arrow pierced into the side of the building for weeks before we finally retrieved it. God said shoot the arrow, proclaim My deliverance over Waterbury. What else could I do?

That was in May of 2004. Two months later the Lord delivered that property into our hands. The arrow of His mighty deliverance had come! On that site we built our 12,400-square-foot Family Life Center where we now minister God's word and provide for His people, young and old. Through Him we turned a derelict, decaying site into a fortification for retaking this city.

As we hear in our prayer closet and are obedient to the Lord, following Him when He directs us, we will see His kingdom advance.

As I've said elsewhere in this book, God also told me to claim the two houses and parking lot next door to our church (they abut the lumber company property). At night I anointed the two houses and the parking lot with oil and dedicated them to the Lord. That began the "prayer fight" I've spoken of. Eventually they would provide a home for many of the ministries of our church as well as a much-needed parking lot.

As we hear in our prayer closet and are obedient to the Lord, following Him when He directs us, we will see His kingdom advance. But this is essential: we must have a persevering, faith-filled spirit to see it manifest.

I'll close this chapter on prophetic acts and prayer with one more testimony involving arrows.

God spoke prophetically in the early 1980s through Pastor Coleman Barlow, who founded our church, that a flaming arrow would be shot out from Waterbury and strike Boston.

In September of 2009 we launched out Pastor Elijah Mickelson, our associate pastor, and his wife Stacie to help plant Common Church in downtown Boston. The day we sent them out we shot a flaming arrow to the east of our church, toward Boston, as a simple prophetic act that is even now bringing great impact to the earth.

Don't you know that our Abba is always faithful? Glory to God!

Let us be sensitive to the Holy Spirit. Let us develop that intimacy through prayer, so we can all do every prophetic act He calls us to. Paul says, in Romans 8:14,

> *For as many as are led by the Spirit of God,*
> *these are the sons of God.*

If we'll just obey the Holy Spirit and be led by Him (John 3:1-3), the earth will manifest His kingdom, all for the glory of our God!

6

Prayer, Perseverance and Hebron

And these things we write to you that your joy may be full.

1 John 1:4

When God wants to teach me a truth or take me into my next season, He seems to prefer to wake me out of sleep late at night or early in the morning.

He usually speaks a phrase or a Scripture to my heart. Then I take that truth and study it out until I can clearly articulate what I have received and apply it to my life. Sometimes my spirit receives a revelation from God and my mind has to catch up to what is already percolating in my spirit (1 Corinthians 2:9).

This morning, God spoke the word "Hebron" into my heart.

In 2 Samuel 5:1-5, David is in Hebron where he is anointed a second time to be Israel's king. Great success is coming for David and his army through the covenant he and the elders of Israel established in Hebron. *The Strong's Concordance* defines "Hebron" as "the seat of associations;" other sources define it as "fellowship and communion" and "the binding friendship place."

Who will you purpose to hang around with in *your* Hebron? Who's in your cluster? The people you sit with and fellowship with will make you or break you! Be led by the Spirit because this is the place of divine alignment.

To pray and persevere like David you will need a company of Hebron people in your life – a small and committed core of people who will help each other war in the Spirit, who will take you to their prayer closets and persevere beside you no matter what adversity comes your way. David had his mighty armor bearer Shammah, famous for standing resolute in a bean patch to hold back a small army of marauding Philistines, even when all others had abandoned the ground. Shammah wasn't going to give the devil an inch, let alone a mile. Talk about a warrior with a persevering spirit!

The people you sit with and fellowship with will make you or break you! Be led by the Spirit because this is the place of divine alignment.

As we read in the last chapter, acting in obedience to the will of God releases the kingdom of God on earth. These two practices – prayer and perseverance – must be planted and nurtured and groomed in the life of each believer. In 2 Samuel 5, David not only prayed but he persevered when the relentless Philistines came against him yet again (2 Samuel 5:17,22).

When you are like David and God raises you up to lead, you'll need a covenant core to rise up alongside you. If you do not have a covenant core it will be difficult to persevere,, perhaps even impossible.

Without Aaron and Hur, Moses would not have won the battle in Exodus 17. We know that David had three mighty men in his inner circle, his covenant core. Jesus had three – Peter, James and John – to ascend the Mount of Transfiguration with Him (Matthew 17). Then a larger covenant core bands together: Abraham, Moses, Joshua, Gideon, and Jesus, to name a few, all developed a band of kindred spirits around them.

David reigned seven years in Hebron, constantly battling against Saul's army during these years, and then 33 years in Jerusalem. That's 40 years of effective leadership. (Wow – that's a long time! Let's you and I develop a persevering, 40-year vision for our leadership.)

He did not operate alone. He did not operate with lukewarm brothers. David endured as a mighty, anointed leader because he had mighty, anointed men around him. God wants to take you from your Hebron and launch you out across the whole world. Worldwide is His strategy, but your alignments with the people around you are essential to you being able to persevere and overcome the enemy.

David had 37 mighty men of God, horses ready to run, loyal soldiers who fought and battled with him. A picture of the three mighty men David chose to most closely align himself with – Adino, Eleazar and Shammah – is painted in 2 Samuel 23:8-12. These warriors were his tightest supports on the battlefield. You need a tight core of people, your own Adino, Eleazar and Shammah, to stand with you and fight with you so that you can take spiritual ground and even physical ground.

Taking ground requires prayer and perseverance with a committed core. So many pastors are leaving the ministry* – as many as 1,800 pastors a month in America,

* http://pastoralcareinc.com/WhyPastoralCare/Statistics.php

according to polls – because they are left all alone to battle the enemy in the field. Being all alone may be their own doing, through habit or choice. But it is clear that we need prayer partners to rise up to cover the senior pastor.*

It was a definite "God thing" when my wife Verna and I arrived as guest preachers in January of 1998 at the church we would later lead, that Ida, who had been at this church almost since its beginning, prayed over Verna at the altar. There was an instant connection from day one. Once we came to serve the church full time, it was this woman we asked to be the church's prayer coordinator. That mantle Ida (she is now Pastor Ida) continues to carry with reverence, authority and power and our bond grows in unity and power every year.

In the Gospel of Luke Jesus teaches about prayer and perseverance through this story:

> *Then He spoke a parable to them, that men always ought to pray and not lose heart, saying: "There was in a certain city a judge who did not fear God nor regard man. Now there was a widow in that city; and she came to him, saying, 'Get justice for me from my adversary.' And he would not for a while; but afterward he said within himself, 'Though I do not fear God nor regard man, yet because this widow troubles me I will avenge her, lest by her continual coming*

*Two must-read resources for raising prayer partners: <u>Partners in Prayer</u> by Dr. John Maxwell, Thomas Nelson, 1996, and <u>Prayer Shield</u> by Dr. C. Peter Wagner, Regal Books, 1992

> *she weary me.'" Then the Lord said, "Hear what the unjust judge said. And shall God not avenge His own elect who cry out day and night to Him, though He bears long with them? I tell you that He will avenge them speedily. Nevertheless, when the Son of Man comes, will He really find faith on the earth?"*
>
> Luke 18:1-8

Jesus taught that "men always ought to pray and not lose heart." One definition of the word "ought" is "to be chained to." I like that: we must be chained to our prayer meetings. We must make prayer our number one priority. This widow (the church) kept coming to the judge (God) continually and was just grinding him down. He dispensed justice and judgment because of her persevering spirit.

Jesus spoke of an unjust judge. But we know that our God is a just judge. In verse 7, Jesus speaks the truth of our speedily avenging Father, delivering justice to His elect who are crying out at all hours to Him. As we persevere in prayer, how much more so will our loving and just Father come and fight for us. He will avenge us and destroy every enemy of our souls.

As we persevere in prayer, how much more so will our loving and just Father come and fight for us.

Sometimes when you are praying it doesn't *look* like anything is happening. Do not be fooled. Press onward by faith (2 Corinthians 5:7). Call on your prayer partners.

Together in "symphonia," in one accord prayer, believe not the things your eyes see but the great things unseen! "For the things which are seen are temporary but the things which are not seen are eternal" (2 Corinthians 4:18).

We must take the word of God to the courtroom of Heaven. Doing this as God's righteous children and bringing our requests daily to God is the faith Jesus speaks of in the final verse of our passage from Luke. So I ask you, when the Son of Man comes will He really find faith on the earth? I say emphatically, "YES!" He will indeed find mighty men and women of God like you and me who persevere, crying out day and night to Him.

We must persevere in the promises of God even when it *looks* like nothing is happening. That's how it is clearing land back at my home, which happens to be an old farm. I've got a lot of stray stones in my land. I grab my sledge hammer and start striking some big, gnarly rock that I need to move but can't budge from where it sits. When the sledge just seems to bounce off that craggy rock it *looks* like nothing is happening. But after I strike and I strike, and I strike again, suddenly a crack appears, my adrenalin rises, and with the next swing the stone shatters! God's word, wielded in persevering prayer, is a relentless sledge hammer that breaks the "boulders" in our land into removeable pieces.

Busting a Boulder

Little did I know when I anointed the two houses next door to our church that the fight was on. That's when the bell rang and I was in the ring for Round One.

The houses were occupied by people who were using drugs and having crazy keg parties right next to the church. People were smoking pot and drinking all over the church parking lot on Friday and Saturday nights. Cars would do "smoke shows," burning their tires all across our lot. A few prayer partners and I, for two long years, would "war" in the sanctuary every Saturday night, crying out to God. (I persevere in this practice, praying most Saturday nights in the church before I minister Sunday mornings.)

We could hear the thumping bass from the obnoxious music. We could hear tires screeching. We could hear drunken shouting. But we would not permit the chaos to distract us; in fact, we purposed to be there at those times. We went to prayer and claimed that property for Jesus. Scripture says we have authority over all the powers of the enemy according to Matthew 18:18 and Luke 10:19, so we would cry out on our altar, "Let God arise, let His enemies scatter" (Psalm 68:1).

We don't pray *for* victory but *from* victory!

Even the creation tells the truth, the constellations revealing how the great warrior-hunter Jesus (Orion) has defeated satan (the scorpion, leviathan, the serpent of old, the devil) by shedding His precious blood on the cross at Calvary. It is paid for, done and settled forever. It is from this position of victory we pray. We don't pray *for* victory but *from* victory!

It was during this prayer-filled, two-year persevering

battle that I was visiting my brother, Rob Lilley, having early morning devotions on his back deck on a peaceful summer morning, when God opened my understanding to Psalm 125:3 which says:

> *For the scepter of wickedness shall not rest on the land allotted to the righteous, lest the righteous reach out their hands to iniquity.*

It was another of God's flaming arrows, placed into my hand to shoot at the enemy. I would claim and I would declare in prayer, "Lord don't let the scepter of wickedness rest on this land you allotted to me. Let the ruling power of evil flee, in Jesus' name!"

At the highest pitch of this battle the property owner came to my office one day and got inches from my face, veins throbbing and eyes bulging, screaming to try to intimidate me. (He could have used a Tic-Tac, too.) "You ain't a real pastor! This ain't even a real church!" he shouted. (He was inspired by a demonic spirit; they love to mock, degrade and intimidate people!) Just like the furious Sanballat and Tobiah attempted to mock and intimidate Nehemiah as he rebuilt the wall (Nehemiah Chapter Four), this guy challenged me. He challenged my mandate. In so doing he also challenged my Father.

A short time after this eruption, maybe a month, he became so sick that he could no longer grip the hammer he used every day to make a living. He came back to me and said, "Alright, I'll sell you the houses now. Give me $400,000 and they're yours." To which I replied, "Come talk to me when you're serious."

And our prayers blazed on. The enemy was on the ropes and the roofer was caving in.

A week passed by and there he was again, this time with a different offer. "I'll sell you my houses for $300,000." To which I replied, again, "Come talk to me when you're serious."

More prayers poured out from our elevated position of victory. It was unstoppable and irresistible.

It wasn't but a few days later that he knocked on my door. "I'll sell you my houses for $200,000." This time I said, "You're getting closer, let's work out a deal" and we talked it through, agreed on a God-inspired price, and in short order we signed the title deed to the two houses. (That title deed was the symbolic substance of faith.) All glory to God for giving us those houses – one of which I'm writing this book in.

When your battle heats up, your victory is right around the corner!

I give you this testimony to encourage you in your own persevering prayer war. When your battle heats up your victory is right around the corner! Don't be so close to the victory God has for you only to give up just inches away. Persevere!

7

PRAYER SYSTEMS

...but we will give ourselves continually to prayer and to the ministry of the word.

ACTS 6:4

At this hour in the body of Christ, God is merging the supernatural with the natural.

In Ezekiel's famous vision we see God bringing the bones, the structure, rattling back together before breathing his Spirit into them (Ezekiel 37:1-14). When God comes and breathes upon Adam in the book of Genesis, Adam comes to life. When God's breath, the creative *ruwach* of God, breathes on us today we come alive. That's when we truly start living the abundant life God intends for all believers.

Spirit underpinned by structure makes for a dynamic church. As it takes two wings to fly a plane it takes two "wings" to soar in the heavenlies: the natural wing of structure with the supernatural wing of the Spirit.

Consider your body. God designed it with multiple systems. Your skeletal system prevents you from being an amorphous blob. With your respiratory system you breathe in rhythms to replenish your body with oxygen and rid itself of waste gas. With your immune system your body attacks all cells that are foreign and harmful. God engineered ten major organ systems and we need all of them, and all the lesser systems for that matter, fully functioning to be abundantly healthy and vital. In the body of Christ we, too, need our "systems" to be fully operational, balanced and strong.

You can look at God's church as a living organism with multiple systems. As I see it, based on Scripture, here are the more prominent ones:

1. Prayer system;
2. Evangelism system;
3. Assimilation system;
4. Offering system; and
5. Teaching and discipling system.

Together they make a healthy church; without any one, or without them functioning as designed, the church forfeits its full potential.

Most times when I speak at different churches I find myself talking to the pastor about one system more than any other: the prayer system. I believe the prayer system of your church is the most important system. It is where you open the door to the King of Glory and invite Him into your life, family, church and city.

After our church began implementing a *system* of prayer we started to overcome obstacles that had been blocking the church for at least the previous ten years.

Prayer: The Tiny Nerve that Moves the Hand of God

To encourage you I'll tell you the story of our own

struggle to break the 200-member barrier. We just could not crack it until a few key systems were in place. The chief of these systems is our prayer system. These systems took us a good two years to raise up but once we did, they formed a supernatural hedge of protection around our church.

God told Abram, "I am your shield, your exceedingly great reward" (Genesis 15:1). In Psalm 3:3 the psalmist says, "But you are a shield around me, O LORD; you bestow glory on me and lift up my head." We witnessed these truths in our urban church. And as in Acts 2:47, people came and were being saved daily. Once our church came into one accord we started impacting our city on many levels.

I believe the prayer system in your church is the most important system.

Here is the one-accord prayer system we raised up that took our church to higher levels in Him.

We started corporate praise and prayer on Friday evenings. Our musicians would begin the night with praise music, stirring the atmosphere up, and then we would mix our pastors and ministers in to pray for what God put on our hearts to birth in or pray through. These nights had structure mixed together with spontaneous moves of the Spirit. They were powerful! Sometimes we would be on our faces in the sanctuary. Sometimes we'd just keep praising and worshipping. Sometimes we would war in the heavenlies against the demonic things going on in our city and nation.

After Friday nights became an institution, the goal then became early morning prayer on the five workdays, with five different leaders – like the five smooth stones young David used to fell Goliath. I was led by the Spirit to recruit people who had my heart and could sign on to my vision of prayer. And God, in turn, was faithful to raise up winners and overcomers for His house of prayer. We were passionately hungry for victory!

We began with early morning corporate prayer every Wednesday. We would begin at 7 A.M., reading Scripture for 10 minutes, worshipping for about 15 minutes, then praying for about 30 minutes, and concluding with the leader presenting a brief devotional: it was, and remains, structure but with freedom to flow.

We are not rigid, but we are structured (there's a real difference). Our structure senses the move of the Spirit. Like a healthy skeletal system we are green and flexible enough to bend if we sense Him leading us elsewhere, or calling us deeper into one area.

Our Prayer System

In the hope that laying it out will inspire your own prayer system, here is the structure that defines what we pray throughout the week (you'll note that we have added Saturdays and Sundays):

Monday: We pray that the word that was preached on Sunday morning is applied to people's lives. We pray that first-time guests return and be plugged into the church body.

Tuesday: We pray for unity in our body (Ephesians

4:3), for God to send us the right guest speakers at the right time, for the saints to be equipped to do the work of ministry (Ephesians 4:11-13), and for the devil to have no room to work in our church, city or state (Ephesians 4:27).

Wednesday: Our church has a vision statement, which says, "We are a dynamic, Spirit-filled regional equipping center, winning and training young and old to grow and mature in their relationship with Jesus Christ, and releasing them to impact their world." We pray that our members will get the vision into their spirits and will run in the vision with us as we fulfill it (Habakkuk 2:2).

Thursday: We pray that our leaders be anointed with fresh oil. We pray that no "burnout" occur! And we pray for new laborers to come forth (Matthew 9:36).

Friday: We pray for our Sunday services to be anointed by the Holy Spirit. We pray for the pastors to be filled with fire, for the musicians and praise and worship leaders to be anointed to enter into the Holy place. We pray that the nursery, children's church and the greeters at our doors be raised up in love and joy to pour out on all who talk to them.

Saturday: We pray for marriages and families. We ask God to bless the husbands and wives with a spirit of unity and wisdom to function in their proper roles. We pray for single moms and single dads to be strong in the Lord. We pray that the families undergoing testing and trials overcome whatever they are faced with.

Sunday morning: In our prayer room off the sanctuary we ask that every life be filled with God's glory, and every unsaved person surrender his or her life to Jesus!

I encourage you to develop and then pray different "themes" like this on different days, as you are led or have a need.

We encourage our people to put on the armor of God before they leave their houses and we pray our way through that (Ephesians 6:12-17). We also teach our people in their devotional time to pray through the Old Testament tabernacle articles of Exodus 30, 37 and 38 – candlesticks, show bread, altar of incense, Holy of Holies (the blood of Jesus). And let's not overlook the profound power of the Lord's Prayer.

When I started Wednesday morning prayer that was all we had for the week. After a few months my Associate Pastor took on Friday mornings. We stayed at these two days for about eighteen months. Then we implemented Thursday morning prayer and quickly after that the Monday and Tuesday leaders rose up. After the two years it took to develop a systematic prayer system in our church the Spirit really started to move and flow on a daily basis.

As we give ourselves to prayer and the ministry of the word there will be a multiplication of disciples who will arise and the word of God will spread across our regions (Acts 6:7). God said it, it's the truth.

Don't despise the day of small beginnings, friend! Don't be discouraged by having but one prayer meeting at your church. That is a great place to start, just not a place to settle. Believe God to raise up a prayer meeting at your church every day, led by different leaders.

Beware pastor: you will burn out if you try to lead

every day by yourself. Don't do it! Cry out to God to raise up watchmen on your wall, prayer warriors and intercessors who have a passion to take territory for Christ. We can do it if we raise up the prayer to open up the heavens so that the Spirit of God can flow.

You can do this! Today, if you're standing in a pile of disarray and troubles you can pick yourself up from the rubble and rebuild. The prophet Zechariah encouraged Zerubbabel as he squared off against what looked to his human eyes an insurmountable task and faced incredible discouragement: "'Not by might nor by power, but by My Spirit,' says the Lord of hosts" (Zechariah 4:6). He spoke these words after the temple construction had just lingered there, dormant and without hope, for 14 long years. These words spoke life into a dry place.

You can arise and take Kingdom ground wherever you are if you will raise up your own prayer system.

You can arise and recapture Kingdom ground wherever you are if you will begin to raise up your own prayer system.

8

Personal Prayer Time

My voice you shall hear in the morning, O Lord;
in the morning I will direct it to You, and I will look up.

Psalm 5:3

In Matthew 6:1-18 Jesus taught us three Christian virtues: giving, praying and fasting. In this chapter, as fitting the focus of this book, let's pay close attention to the second virtue, prayer.

Hear in a new, fresh way the words of Jesus – I think of them as prayer strategy number one:

> *But you, when you pray, go into your room, and when you have shut your door, pray to your Father who is in the secret place; and your Father who sees in secret will reward you openly.*
>
> Matthew 6:6

Prayer is any believer's number one priority. If you are a full-time minister you especially need to place prayer at the top of your job description, like the early apostles who said, "We will give ourselves to prayer and the ministry of the word" (Acts 6:4).

Notice that the verse says "*we*." There needs to be corporate agreement in our churches of what it means when we say, "We will give ourselves to prayer and the word." And you, pastor, must spend time praying over your people and church ministries daily.

Prayer time must be plugged into your calendar strategically. Once plugged in, don't unplug it. Don't let the press of time or other people's agendas unplug it. Without frequent, regular prayer times you will take no new ground in your life, and your church will take no new ground in your town or city.

Prayer time must be plugged into your calendar strategically.

Mark 1:35 presents one of the pictures we have of just how Jesus went about praying. Jesus is our teacher, our example:

> *Now in the morning, having risen a long while before daylight, He went out and departed to a solitary place; and there He prayed.*

As I said earlier in Chapter 2, there is breakthrough power when you pray every day:

1. At the same time – *"in the morning…a long while before daylight;"*

2. In the same place – *"a solitary place;"*

3. With a plan – *"Thy kingdom come, Thy will be done."*

Wake up in the morning with the mind of an invader. Execute your battle plan. Command the day!

We must begin every day in the place of prayer where the keys are. This is how the righteous become filled with the power of the Spirit to live in victory all day long. Jesus arose in the dark, a great while before daybreak and the rush of the day and went to a quiet place. David said in Psalm 5:3,

> *My voice you shall hear in the morning, O Lord; in the morning I will direct it to You, and I will look up.*

In the Hebrew the word for "direct" can also be translated as "to set a battle formation." The place of prayer is where God sets victory for us over every weapon of the enemy. No weapon formed against us shall prosper when we assemble in the war room of the Lord.

We must begin every day in the place of prayer where the keys are.

Praying God's Word in Your Personal Prayer Time

A devotion plan will help empower your prayer life. There is no better strategic plan than reading your Bible in harmony with your prayer life. In John 15:7 Jesus reveals another truth:

> *If you abide in Me, and My words abide in you, you will ask what you desire, and it shall be done for you.*

So we must "weld" together prayer and the word of God, like "the twelve" in the early church in Acts 6:4:

> *...but we will give ourselves continually to prayer and to the ministry of the word.*

It is in times of solitude, just you and the Spirit, that He will illuminate a specific passage of Scripture and transform it into a *rhema* word for your life – revelation straight from the heart of the Father. *Revelation* leads to *impartation; impartation* leads to *life transformation.*

It is with that *rhema* word I pray and believe what God has promised me will come to pass. This is the sword of the Spirit. This is how we can cut through the heavenlies.

God spoke to evangelist Reinhard Bonnke, saying, "My word in your mouth is as powerful as My word in My mouth. The power is in the word!"* Praying the word is a mighty, effective and fiery tool of faith that advances God's kingdom.

Every time I am ready for my next season God is faithful to supply a revelatory word that pulls me into that season. Isaiah 55:10,11 says,

> *For as the rain comes down, and the snow from heaven,*
> *And do not return there,*
> *But water the earth,*
> *And make it bring forth and bud,*

* www.supernaturalsigns.com/2009/01/20/reinhard-bonnke/

That it may give seed to the sower
And bread to the eater,
So shall My word be that goes forth from
My mouth;
It shall not return to Me void,
But it shall accomplish what I please,
And it shall prosper in the thing for
which I sent it.

Receiving God's word that comes from His mouth (including the *rhema* word for your specific situation) will do something in your life; it will not return barren and fruitless, a waste of God's time, so to speak. No, it will accomplish God's will in the earth. This is the power that causes things to bud and grow.

I have been meditating on Psalm 37 and declaring specific portions of it over my world. I stand in faith and await the transformation that is on its way. I speak it out loud. Sometimes I speak it very loudly. Your words are spirit and life! They have power to kill or resurrect, hurt or heal, sever or reconcile.

I encourage you to frame your world with His word (Hebrews 11:3). If you frame it with anything else it will be too small!

In the way a marinade releases flavor, softens toughness to tenderness and transforms the bland into the sumptuous, your prayer time will benefit if you marinate it.

The recipe for "prayer marinade" is God's awesome presence with equal parts of reading His word, hearing His voice and declaring His word. Pray this way and you will see delicious results in the heavenly and earthly realms.

Getting back to *rhema* words, God assures you and me in 1 Timothy 1:18 that by these prophetic words spoken to us, with faith, we wage a good warfare. But if you put aside your prayer faith and a good conscience you'll suffer a shipwreck. The waves of this life will run you aground.

Do you have a strategic plan for reading your Bible? Have a journal and pen sitting next to you as you read and He speaks to you, to record your insights from God. Maybe a devotional book will stir your soul. But you need to come up with a plan for marinating in the word. With no strategy there is no big victory.

The recipe for "prayer marinade:" God's awesome presence with equal parts of reading His word, hearing His voice and declaring His word.

We are certain from Romans 10:17 that faith comes by hearing and hearing by the word of God. Faith comes by hearing – *and hearing and hearing and hearing!* In your prayer closet listen to God's word daily for daily faith. You must hear God's word of instruction for each season of your life.

Doubt comes by hearing the word of men. Guard your ears! Take stock. Be aware of what you're feeding on. Sadly it's too easy to slide back into old habits and let the world's way of speaking and thinking sneak back into your heart and mind. Watch for it, take authority over it and cast it into the "That's Not Me Anymore" trash bin.

Yes, we all grow in power and authority when we read the word and then meditate on it daily (Joshua 1:8). "Meditate" means to speak and mutter with your mouth. I used to think meditating was exclusively a quiet activity. It's not. Read and pray the word of God out loud. It is not enough to just think it and be quiet, you should speak it! Vocalizing the word of God back to Him is another key to overcoming, fruitful prayer.

In your faithful prayer time God will send his word to you and pull you into your next season. But it only comes to those who seek Him with faith and expect it (Hebrews 11:6). That is the way God has been taking me from faith to faith and glory to glory: by His proceeding word! Deuteronomy 8:3 says, "Man does not live by bread alone but by every word that proceeds from the mouth of God." Catch that proceeding word today!

Doubt comes by hearing the word of men.

Jesus used the word of God as a sword against the old adversary in Matthew 4:4:

> *But He answered and said, "It is written, 'Man shall not live by bread alone, but by every word that proceeds from the mouth of God.'"*

The word "proceeds" in the Greek – *ekporeuomai* – translates as "to go forth, to cut forward a way." Now THAT is how you advance forward for the Lord: by receiving the word that is coming from the mouth of the Lord! It is strong and mighty. It is a weapon ready for you to use. Listen in the prayer closet as you read your Bible. As you dig into God's word His Holy Spirit is going to speak to you. Read God's word every single day and let God speak revelation into your spirit so it becomes a *rhema* word. And listen.

Slow down. Make time to listen to God's word speaking to you. He that has an ear let him hear what the Spirit is saying!

When Israel did not listen to God, God permitted a chastening:

> *So He humbled you, allowed you to hunger, and fed you with manna which you did not know nor did your fathers know, that He might make you know that man shall not live by bread alone; but man lives by every word that proceeds from the mouth of the LORD.*
>
> DEUTERONOMY 8:3

This Hebrew word translated here as "proceeds" – *motsa* – means "going forth, exit, a source, a fountain, a gate, rising expectation, a mine, a meadow, brought out." This is key to your breakthrough in the situation you're facing. Only by the word of God are you going to move forward and exit into your new promised land!

This passage from Deuteronomy references Exodus 16:16-35 where God fed the children of Israel with manna faithfully every day for 40 long years. God taught the children of Israel four things about manna as described in those verses; each has a lesson for you and me today:

1. *Every person gather an omer of manna for your household.* Get bread at your prayer time to eat, and then feed your house with it.

2. *The manna is to be eaten daily with nothing left over.* You need to eat God's word every day. Eat the bread which symbolizes Christ (John 6:35,41). Eat all of the Lamb!

3. *On the sixth day, the day before the Sabbath, gather two portions.* Prepare your heart with plenty on Saturday so you are able to make Sunday a refreshing Sabbath rest for you and your family.

4. *No baking on the Sabbath.* It's time to enter into God's rest (Psalm 37:7) and cease laboring (Hebrews 4, Luke 10:35-42). Sit at Jesus' feet and just receive His life-giving, restoring word. If you are naturally a Martha, this is your time to supernaturally become a Mary.

Prayer alone with Jesus is the foundation stone of prayer. It is where you eat His manna (Exodus 16), drink His living water (Exodus 17:1-7) and rest in the victory of Jehovah-nissi (Exodus 17:8-16)!

Don't strive in your own strength like Martha but rest in His presence and hear His word like Mary, for this is eternal and will never be taken away from you.

The key is in the closet. Enjoy your prayer closet

time. Look forward to it. Relish it. Let it refresh and recharge you. God is about ready to pull you into your next season by His word *so get ready*!

9

Committed Prayer Partners

And Aaron and Hur supported his hands, one on one side, and the other on the other side....

Exodus 17:12

After you lay the foundation stone of praying alone, the way Jesus did often, one-on-one with His Heavenly Father, you need the balance and strength of praying with others. I think of it as prayer strategy number two.

Because you are a part of the body of Christ you cannot expect a vibrant prayer life as a lone ranger. Other faith-filled, Spirit-filled believers like you will "touch and agree" with you in prayer. Your prayers will be amplified as you agree with another kindred spirit (Matthew 18:18-20). With a tenacious faith in the Rock one believer can put 1,000 enemies to flight and two can scatter 10,000 (Deuteronomy 32:30). Great odds, I'd say!

We read in Matthew 17 that Jesus had Peter, James and John as His inner circle prayer triad. When you agree in prayer (Matthew 18:19) you invite the presence of God to come into your midst (Matthew 18:20). The Greek word for "agree" in vs. 19 is *symphoneo* which means, "to sound together, be in accord, be in harmony." We derive the English word symphony from *symphoneo,* the blending and amplification of instruments to make a powerful, harmonized, beautiful sound.

As Moses had Aaron and Hur lift up His arms in a prayer triad so that Joshua would prevail in his battle over the Amalakites down in the valley (Exodus 17:8-16), God erects a supernatural hedge of protection over your ministry as you raise up your prayer partners.

Get together with your prayer partners to make the same sound in prayer and watch your requests be answered by our Father in Heaven. When two or three are in unity there God manifests by His Spirit; when unity flows in a prayer meeting fresh oil flows down on the head and to every part of the body (Psalm 133). It is in this unity of brethren spirits that God commands the blessings of heaven on us.

God erects a supernatural hedge of protection over your ministry as you raise up your prayer partners.

Get together at least once a month and share your vision with them. Then make the same sound together in intercession. It will only be a matter of time and timing before your vision manifests!

When God showed Moses how to build the mercy seat, He said there were to be two angels, not one. In Isaiah 6 we see a picture of the seraphim flying about the throne of grace crying, "Holy, holy, holy is the LORD of hosts" in His manifested presence. When we cry in unity with one another, "Holy, holy, holy," God manifests himself in the midst of our praise (Psalm 22:3).

Evangelist Charles Finney understood this supernatural principle. Finney was a mighty man of God. He was powerfully used by God all across the United States in the 1800s revival called the Second Great Awakening and was referred to as the father of modern revivalism. But not so well known were Finney's two prayer partners, Daniel Nash and Abel Cleary. With Finney they formed a prayer triad.

These two intercessory prayer warriors accompanied Finney, often preceding him to a town or city where a revival meeting was scheduled so they could pray in advance, loosening the soil and storming the gates from their rented rooms. While Finney preached in the glory of God these two men together would war in the spirit. Such was their support and their interconnectedness to each other and to God that when Nash and Cleary passed away, Finney ceased his revival preaching across the country and settled down to pastor a small church in upstate New York.

I can't wait to read the chapter in the *Chronicles of Heaven* on the lifestyles of Daniel Nash and Abel Cleary! Just picture it: those two prayed down the kingdom everywhere they went. They brought fresh wind and fresh fire to the earth through their agreeing, *symphoneo* prayer. And that is what we are to do to see holy fire fall in our regions!

We have four prayer partners who have lifted up my arms and my wife's arms since 1998: Minister Todd and Marcello, and Pastor Ida and Minister Vivian. These powerful prayer warriors have refreshed and renewed us more times than we can count. During our Sunday services other mighty men and women of God whom Pastor Ida and Minister Vivian have raised up gather in our upper room – a second-floor room that overlooks our sanctuary. They intercede for God to move on each person at the service. We continually see the Holy Spirit change hearts and lives because of the prayer agreement of our prayer warriors.

Finding Your Prayer Partners

David was mighty because he had mighty men of faith and courage around him. He and his men performed great exploits for God (1 Chronicles 11:19). God will surely manifest as harmonious prayers rise up. We encourage our people to find a kindred spirit and pray daily with that person, to make the same sound in prayer. And I encourage you.

We continually see the Holy Spirit change hearts and lives because of the prayer agreement of our prayer warriors.

Jesus prayed, all night long, and only then did he choose his twelve disciples. Following Jesus' example, we should take great care and use divine discernment when looking for prayer partners.

Because prayer fosters deep intimacy between prayer partners, men should look for men and women for women – that is the first step in the search.

You should already be (or start) praying with that person in an "unofficial" role. If you are looking to begin a prayer relationship with an eye to prayer partnership, keep it loose to begin with. If your spirits connect and there is a wonderful flow of the Spirit when you two start to pray then you've found a key to your next level – your prayer partner. Look out devil, this is the way we will destroy your works (1 John 3:8). Be a taker and a breaker!

I thank God for raising up mighty warriors around me, faithful men and women with whom we share our needs, like Ministers Al, Mary, Vivian, and Doris, and Linda, Diane, Jennifer, Livina, Dawn and Cynthia, to name only a few in our house. These faithful prayer partners birth-in the needs we are seeing and sensing in the Kingdom of God. These warriors do not replace our own personal prayer time, they magnify it.

We encourage our people to find a prayer partner ... and pray daily with that person, to make the same sound in prayer. And I encourage you.

I thank God for others like Fanny, Dana and Desiree who have prayed daily for nine years and impacted one of Waterbury's harshest neighborhoods. These three women of faith have driven the enemy back from 18 different streets and brought peace to the children of Crownbrooke. With great joy they have given Christmas and Easter parties for the children, handing out gifts and toys, and sharing Jesus with each child. It reminds me of the overcoming saints in Hebrews 11:33 "who through faith subdued kingdoms, worked righteousness, obtained promises, stopped the mouths of lions…."

I thank God for Minister Ana who has distributed more than 600 shoe boxes overflowing with gifts at a public elementary school these past six years. Each child receives the love of Jesus and warm smiles from Ana and her team. They will forever be impacted by God's love through Ana and her team, a team that grows larger every year (Matthew 5:16).

I thank God for Minister Angie, Clif, Minister Doris, Betty, Minister Vivian and Phil who devote themselves to the food pantry where hundreds of families are fed each and every month.

I thank God for Marcelo whose exploits of love on the streets win the lost and broken people of Waterbury to Christ on a daily basis.

Friend, raise up *symphoneo* prayer partners and then move in the direction of the sounds of Heaven.

I thank God for Minister Todd and his wife, Janet, and Minister Debbie and their missionary hearts. Through a church building project in Ghana and the steady support of orphanages and hospitals there and in Kenya, they have impacted Africa in the name of Jesus.

I could go on and on about the warriors God has raised up here at our great church. Please receive this in the spirit of humility in which it is intended: I call our church "great" because prayer partners are rising up praying, faithfully and with the conviction of victory, and then moving in obedience to their prayers.

Wherever your ministry and church is today, agree together with God who calls things that are not yet as though they are now! Friend, raise up *symphoneo* prayer partners and then move in the direction of the sounds of

Heaven. When you do this you advance God's kingdom with joy and love (Zechariah 4:6).

You need prayer partners to spiritually survive and thrive – without Aaron and Hur holding up Moses' arms on the hilltop, Joshua would have lost in the valley. Let's pray, "Oh God, raise up prayer partners for us so that together we can advance Your kingdom in our city!"

10

THE POWER OF ONE-ACCORD PRAYER MEETINGS

So when they heard that, they raised their voice to God with one accord....

ACTS 4:24

The power of one accord prayer meetings among believers is truly staggering. Deuteronomy 32:30 tells us that one can put 1,000 to flight, and two can scatter 10,000 demons. There is a supernatural synergy that is released like a bomb in the spirit realm when believers come together in one accord prayer.

When the church comes together to pray in one accord the warrior bride advances the kingdom of God at the speed of light. This is the place you rule over; this is where you crush the enemy (see Psalm 110:1-4, the psalm most often quoted in the New Testament).

Acts 1:14 records how the church was birthed out of a one-accord prayer meeting:

> *These all continued with one accord in prayer and supplication, with the women and Mary the mother of Jesus, and with His brothers.*

The Greek word for "one accord" is *homothumadon,* which means "two of the same kind, together." It means having the same mind, the same vision, the same heart and the same spirit. Watch for the power of praying with believers who have the same mindset, the same vision and the same spirit as you. When you begin praying with them the Spirit of God starts working in you and through you. This is when the kingdom of God manifests in your midst rapidly.

When the body that is the church comes into one-accord prayer meetings you better stand back! Just look at what happened in the Book of Acts:

- Acts 1:8 – Jesus promised supernatural ability to witness in Jerusalem (locally), Judea (regionally), Samaria (nationally) and the uttermost parts of the world (globally);
- Acts 1:14 – the purposes of the church were birthed;
- Acts 2:1-4 – the fire of the Spirit came and filled each believer;
- Acts 2:47 – the Lord added to the church daily those who were being saved;
- Acts 4:24 – when persecution arose they responded with a one-accord prayer meeting;
- Acts 4:31 – things in the heaven and earth realms literally shook (breakthroughs); all were filled afresh with the Spirit (fresh anointing); they spoke the word of God with boldness (evangelism); and
- Acts 5:12-16 – signs and wonders happened in the atmosphere of a one-accord praying church.

If you want to learn how to change your town or city just meditate on the Book of Acts: the early church won 20,000 of the 60,000 souls in Jerusalem to Christ within 20 years. Wow! And we can do the same wherever God has planted us! There will be growth in your church when you pray together in one accord.

When the church of today starts to pray you can expect the seven marks of the early church we just reviewed to manifest. There will be a dynamic and fresh Holy Spirit empowerment of the saints. It was our joy, for example, just last week to see a harvest of 15 new converts to Christ who were baptized and received the Lord. The Holy Spirit moved in power as each one, young and seasoned alike, testified to what Christ had done and was doing in their lives.

If you want to learn how to change your town or city just meditate on the Book of Acts.

I outlined our prayer calendar in Chapter 7. Our vision now is to claim perpetual seamless prayer, 24 hours a day, 7 days a week, 365 days a year in our prayer room. (*Amen! Do it Lord Jesus!*) We want to make God's house a house of prayer for all nations (Isaiah 56:7). It's time for the church to birth the kingdom of God from heaven into the earth on our knees. The only way it will come is through one-accord prayer meetings.

Prayer Shuts Them Down

I told you earlier about how prayer was so key to

cleaning up our city. Waterbury had a dozen busy brothels fronting as massage parlors. They were a great concern to us. One den, in fact, was not even half a mile from our doors. Like King Josiah, my heart is to see the spirit of prostitution ground to powder (2 Kings 23:7)! So we went to God in unified prayer, and in those prayer times God showed us that we needed to propose and pass new by-laws in our city that would tightly regulate the opening of any such massage businesses.

We went to meetings at city hall, talked to the city planner and gave him model by-laws. The city passed new zoning laws because of the church and because of one-accord prayer.

But the Lord wasn't through just yet. While we continued to pray in one accord, God put it into the chief of police's heart to investigate what was really going on in these strongholds of satan (as if we all did not already know). On one Friday night, different undercover police officers went into each of these businesses, arresting many women for prostitution. It was all over the papers, television and internet. The Lord closed down every one of those 12 prostitution dens in one night. They would never open again.

Locking and Releasing

> *The key of the house of David I will lay on his shoulder; so he shall open, and no one shall shut; and he shall shut, and no one shall open.*
>
> ISAIAH 22:22

THROUGH UNIFIED, ONE-ACCORD PRAYER *God gave Pastor James and his prayer warriors His strategy for the steps that would shut down a dozen thriving houses of prostitution in Waterbury. Here Pastor James stands on the rubble of one of those houses.*

I believe that this is the key of the house of David: to praise and pray under the anointing of the Holy Spirit and by so doing lock up the heavens so evil cannot operate. This is the Davidic anointing that we believers should covet and pursue. When we deploy this type of praise, worship and one-accord prayer we will witness the Holy Spirit work in power. We will see all demonic spirits flee like they did from Saul when David played his harp (1 Samuel 16:23).

Friend, you and your one-accord prayer partners can stop demonic activity no matter what the level in the civil realm: local, regional, national or global. This is the power and authority we have in Jesus' name. Glory to God for all the families that the Lord will save through you because of this authority.

I thank God for the power of one-accord prayer meetings because they jolt and shake the heavenly and earthly realms and usher the Spirit actively near for a move of the Almighty!

11

PRAYER, FASTING AND "SUDDENLIES"

And a threefold cord is not quickly broken.

ECCLESIASTES 4:12

Jesus said, in Matthew 17:21, after casting a demon out of a young boy, "...this kind does not go out except by prayer and fasting." He was revealing that there are certain strongholds in the spirit realm that will only move when a person prays and fasts.

There is a supernatural release of power when you pray and fast. In fasting you humble your soul (Psalm 35:13) and release the power of God through your acts of obedience (Isaiah 58:6-12).

When the Holy Spirit speaks a new word into our lives during times of fasting we try to be obedient to that word. During a recent fast, for example, God spoke to my spirit, "Walk before me with clean hands and a pure heart" (Psalm 24:4). I meditated on that word. I turned it over and over, filtering my thoughts through it and fleshing it out. I travelled to new levels by evaluating my motives and to what I was putting my hands. I asked God to reveal if every one of my daily activities pleased Him. I re-surrendered my hands and heart to the King.

Another "theme" of that fast was "ears to hear what the Spirit is saying" (Mark 4:24, Revelation 2:7). Fasting weakens your flesh and sensitizes your spirit to hear better.

Every January since 2005 we have entered into a 21-day fast as a church body. Each year we've seen more of our members invest themselves into it so that now we have a mighty army that prays and fasts. It's a precious time to press into the Father. We hold sessions in our prayer room each of those 21 days at seven A.M. and seven P.M.. We examine our lives and re-orchestrate them to walk in His will. We witness so many amazing breakthroughs on personal, family and corporate levels.

Some years we have agreed to pray and fast together for 40 days. In 2006, for example, we went on a 40-day corporate fast as a church and I personally went deeper with the Lord by denying my flesh for 40 days with water and juice only. As I lived on liquids the Spirit of God came into my life and ministry in a fresh way. I received a new anointing to preach and pray. My life and ministry became fresh and alive again. God made "all things new" for me. New wine in new wine skins is a promise to the Christian who prays and fasts (Mark 2:18-22), like Jesus when he returned from fasting 40 days (Luke 4:14): He came back to town "in the power of the Spirit."

If you've lost your edge in the spirit and you need to sharpen your saw, prayer and fasting are going to do it.

If you've lost your first love it's time to fast. If you've lost your passion to minister it's time to fast. If you've lost your edge in the spirit and you need to sharpen your saw, prayer and fasting are going to do it.

Our flesh man is a spoiled, rotten baby. He always

lives for the here and now, never considering the future or the consequences. We need to stay all over him or he will get out of control. Left unchecked our flesh will gorge on "the lust of the flesh, the lust of the eyes and the pride of life" (1 John 2:16). Feeding our spirit more than feeding our flesh's desires makes us powerful spiritual pipelines. All great spiritual awakenings have happened thru people who prayed and fasted.

God describes His chosen fast in Isaiah 58: 6-12. It is the type of fast God is pleased with. When you pray and fast you build places, impact generations and restore desolations (Isaiah 58:12 and 61:4). Jesus is giving the nations and the generations to people who pray and fast.

Fasting – depriving our strong, habitual, carnal desires – makes us freer and freer in Christ.

As we give ourselves to physical fasting it opens the door of our spirit to the purposes and plans God has designed for us. This is the "higher realm" of fasting into which our Father desires to transfer us. It's in this realm God undoes bonds of wickedness lodged deep within our minds and souls (Isaiah 58:6). These are strongholds that satan and the world have stuck inside us. They're sticky and they hang on, but true fasting – depriving our strong, habitual, carnal desires – makes us freer and freer in Christ, and what a place of power that is. Then out of this liberty of spirit we reach out and touch other people and every yoke breaks! It's the anointing of the Holy Spirit that we welcome in during our prayer and fasting time that shatters every yoke (Isaiah 10:27).

Praying, Fasting and Giving

Scripture teaches us that there are three habits or virtues every Christian must develop. Jesus revealed the three as written in Matthew 6: giving (v.2), praying (v.6) and fasting (v.16). We should develop these disciplines as a believer in Christ. When we mix all three together we walk in the fullness of our destiny.

This is the three-fold cord of the Spirit written of in Ecclesiastes (4:11-13). This is the 30-, 60- and 100-fold process that comes to life when you make it a lifestyle to give, pray and fast. Live this lifestyle and you will manifest God's 100-fold blessings in your life.

Giving is a powerful, supernatural discipline that complements fasting and prayer. I believe it has such power because, like fasting, it brings into check our habit of being selfish, even greedy. Giving calls us higher. Giving also releases the blessings of God into our lives (Malachi 3:10). It breaks the curse of poverty.

Jesus reveals a spiritual truth in Luke 6:38: whatever measure we use to give to God is what is going to be used to measure back to us. It's like a spiritual boomerang. If you are stingy and miserly, hoarding your "hard earned" money, He will give you that same portion back; if you are generous with Him you can expect that He will fill your house with plenty and your spirit with new wine (Proverbs 3:10).

There are breakthroughs that can only happen when people pray and fast – not praying without fasting or fasting without praying. In our church there were certain, stubborn spiritual walls erected by the enemy over time that came down *only* as we prayed and fasted in one accord as a body of believers.

We are also seeing this truth work in our city. As we pray and fast, God is touching the impoverished Crownbrook neighborhood of Waterbury. We are seeing many strongholds being ripped down. We are seeing families come to Christ. We are seeing a peace settle over a hostile neighborhood. We are seeing drug dens shutting down and hopeful people restoring once-handsome houses across this once infested area of our city. Wow! Jesus really is a restorer of streets to dwell in even today! This kind of dramatic redemption happens through those people who are willing to pray and fast for God's glory.

Giving also releases the blessings of God into our lives. It breaks the curse of poverty.

At the beginning of 2010 we were deeded an old house free and clear in that same Crownbrook neighborhood. We will begin remodeling the old house and will use it to impact families in that neighborhood. We envision it as a headquarters to our church's outreach to God's children in that neighborhood. This was another "suddenly" that God just seems to delight in doing. Not surprisingly, it came right after our 21-day, first fruits fast in January. You've got to love it! (And "way to go" warriors Dana, Desiree and Fanny!)

Feeling Dry? It's Fast Time!

When you feel dry and you've lost your passion for ministry it's time for a fast.

Jesus taught that after He ascended into heaven, His bride would fast, and as she fasts new wine would be put into new wineskins:

> *But the days will come when the bridegroom will be taken away from them, and then they will fast in those days. No one sews a piece of unshrunk cloth on an old garment; or else the new piece pulls away from the old, and the tear is made worse. And no one puts new wine into old wineskins; or else the new wine bursts the wineskins, the wine is spilled, and the wineskins are ruined. But new wine must be put into new wineskins.*
>
> MARK 2:20-22

New anointing has to be poured into flexible people because flexible people can carry out the will of Heaven. Have you considered this process? In order to create a fresh, supple wineskin an animal must die to forfeit the hide to make that new wineskin. In the same way there has to be someone who will die to self and die to their carnal man in order to contain fresh, new spiritual life. To be carnally minded – to let the flesh drive us, to hang onto old habits and ways, to elevate ourselves over others – is a living death. To be spiritually minded and renewed is life and peace (Romans 8:6).

This is the desire of Jesus for you and me. When we pray and fast and soak in His presence God kindly kills our flesh and fills up our spirit with the Bread of Life. Then we go forward and share what He has given us. Each gospel records many miracles, but there is only one told in all four: the feeding of the five thousand. I believe God's greatest desire for His bride today is that we would feed the thronging multitudes everywhere with the Bread of Life.

Jesus said, "Unless a grain of wheat falls into the ground and dies, it remains alone; but if it dies, it produces much grain" (John 12:24). When Jesus died he was the kernel of wheat that produced a magnificent harvest. Out of grain you make bread. Jesus is the Bread of Life, daily bread by which we live. His desire is to feed the whole world His word.

When you combine prayer and fasting you can expect the Lord to move in "suddenlies."

It Could Only Be You, Lord!

And, by the way, when you combine prayer with fasting you can expect the Lord to move in "suddenlies," those super-quick changes that can only be supernatural.

In January of 2010, in the middle of our 21-day, first fruits fast, I had the joyless duty of sending out a letter to the families with children in Lighthouse Christian Academy that told them that if we didn't have a $30,000 miracle within two weeks we would be forced to close the doors. (In the middle of the corporate fast – funny timing, right?)

The next day little Emmanuel, a kindergartener, came into the school with an envelope containing 22 cents that he had saved, and he asked, "Will this help keep my school open?" That triggered faith in everyone who heard it! It was like the firing pin that touched off another suddenly of God.

God spoke to me saying, *"This ministry will rise or fall according to its level of prayer."*

The students rallied and brought in their piggy banks and dumped out their change into the offering baskets at the altar. My sons, James and John, brought their Red Sox banks and gave all their money to the Lord. Two local news channels came by to film a segment on the school. Several local businesses contributed. The day after our church-wide fast ended a woman (who was not a member of our congregation) came to our offices and blessed the Lighthouse Christian Academy with a $3,000 gift. Our church also gave a generous love offering. Through it all God worked to keep the Lighthouse Christian Academy open. Wow – the miracles that flow when people pray, fast and seek God!

The week after that same fast Verna and I received an unexpected check in the mail which blessed us.

And let me tell you how we received our horses! We live on a property that was an old farm, Verna grew up with horses in South Dakota, and our twelve-year-old

Jedidiah wanted to have a horse. We were ripe for one.

So my family and I agreed in prayer during the fast that the Lord would provide us with one. Jedi and I would pray in the evenings for God to send not just any horse, but the right horse. One day after our 21-day fast in September ended we received a call from a friend. He told us that his friend, whom we did not know, wanted to give us a horse *and* a pony plus saddles, brushes, tack, buckets – all we needed to raise them.

This is all clearly the favor of God (Psalm 5:12) and I'll tell you this: God's favor is more precious to me than anything else in life.

Friend, prayer and fasting is the atomic bomb of the Spirit. It will obliterate any wall that old serpent builds.

Here's one more "suddenly story" to glorify God and show how prayer and fasting change the atmosphere. When we came to First Assembly of God in 1998, on April 26, God spoke to us these three things: love the people, they've been thru a lot, teach the people to pray, and clean the building.

Saying our church building was in rough shape would be a real understatement. It was a rambling old banquet hall well past its prime. It had a leaky roof and carpeting that stunk of mold and who knows what else. It was funky. The sound system squealed. Outside, people would dump their broken furniture and bulky trash behind the church in the dirt and tar parking lot, which was thoroughly overtaken by weeds I might add. It got so bad that our Assemblies of God district office put a "for sale" sign on the property in December of 1997 that was still there when we arrived. We needed God to turn this dismal ship around.

Then we had our "suddenly." As our leadership team was praying and fasting for three days, the Holy Spirit gave witness that the back of our church would be cleaned up and an old building on our property would be demolished. We said "Yes Lord!" and received it in faith.

Don't you know that just a week later a man came by whom we didn't know but who owned a demolition company and said he would do it for the Lord. Talk about a Holy Ghost wrecking ball! He tore off the decrepit old kitchen, knocked down two buildings and jack hammered up all the cracked concrete (which, because of all the re-pouring over the years to counter the sinking and sagging buildings, was about two feet thick and made for a monumental task). He even hauled it all away!

Believe that when you fast and pray you will release the supernatural hand of God into your circumstances.

That was a historic day in our church, glory to God! The job was estimated at $35,000 to $45,000 by other companies but this man on a mission did the work for just $6,500.

Friend, believe that when you pray and fast you will release the supernatural hand of God into your circumstances.

Jesus said "prayer *and* fasting." If you just fast and do not pray nothing will happen except you will lose a pound or two. (Jentezen Franklin says that fasting without praying is just heavy-duty dieting – I love that!) Your fasting must be mixed with spending time in the closet where the key is, seeking God's plans for your life. If you seek Him you will find Him (Matthew 7:7). The seeker gets everything from God! He who asks receives, and he who doesn't ask, doesn't receive (James 4:2). I love seeking after the promises of God! And I fully trust in His word that says He rewards those who diligently seek Him (Hebrews 11:6).

People who pray and fast establish the government and order of God. So let's go for it! Let's pay the price for the anointing. Let's push down our flesh, push back the lust of the world and pray and fast until God's kingdom is established in our churches. When you ignite the atomic bomb of the Spirit through prayer and fasting expect the "suddenlies" of God!

Strategies for Fasting

Here are some tips that help me stay on track when I enter into a fast:

1. *Get a friend to fast with you.* Hold each other accountable and pray together every day. Expect to reach new heights.

2. *Meditate on the Scriptures.* Let the Holy Spirit minister to your heart. Be intentional: slow down and meditate on the Scripture God speaks to your heart.

3. *Journal the insights God gives you during your*

fast. Insights are going to flow in this special season of pushing down the flesh to let your spirit arise. Write them down. Then go back and meditate on these insights and apply them so they make a difference in your daily life; otherwise, they are just insights.

4. *Drink a fasting drink and plenty of water.* It will purge the toxins that have lodged themselves in your body over the months. Here's a simple recipe for a potent but palatable drink that I use:

1 gallon (3.8l) water

1 cup (236ml) lemon juice

1 cup (120ml) pure maple syrup

¼ teaspoon (large pinch) cayenne pepper

12

Praying in the Spirit

I thank my God I speak with tongues more than you all....

1 Corinthians 14:18

Praying in the Spirit is a spiritual exercise and a discipline through which we enter the spirit realm where God dwells.

The realm of the spirit is, for lack of a better word, so "huge" that it is beyond the capability of our intellect to truly grasp. Consider that scientists estimate as many as 400 billion stars make up the Milky Way Galaxy, where you and I inhabit one lovely but definitely tiny planet. God created many more galaxies like our own Milky Way – more than 350,000,000,000 of them.

Wow! Our creative Daddy is so big and yet He tends to us! This is exactly what David marvelled over in Psalm 8:3,4:

> *When I consider Your heavens, the work of Your fingers,*
> *The moon and the stars, which You have ordained,*
> *What is man that You are mindful of him,*
> *And the son of man that You visit him?*

And our galaxy just keeps on expanding, even at an accelerating rate, and new stars keep on appearing. The creative power of God's word is still at work! When we pray in the Spirit we enter the amazing greatness of God Who is always creating. As God is a creator-expander so then we become creator-expanders.

As we pray in the Spirit we enter into the realm of the Spirit, the place where God dwells. In the Spirit realm we discover new attributes of God. Like the scientists who explore with the revealing power of the Hubble Space Telescope and seem to continually uncover new dimensions of our universe, in a similar way we receive new revelations as we give ourselves to praying in the Spirit. It is fresh manna, made in God's throne room, and it changes our spirits. As we see the new-to-us attributes of our Father, we can only cry out like God's burning ones, "Holy, holy, holy is the Lord of Hosts!"

When we pray in the Spirit we enter into the amazing greatness of God Who is always creating.

But if we chose to remain in our own finite human intellect we merely orbit in our own little worlds and pay scant attention to the infinite greatnesss of God – quite ironic considering many of us live in places like America and Europe where the "culture of the mind" is elevated with pride, as it was in Athens in Paul's day. For many on this planet today, everything has to be filtered through the limitations of the intellect. It becomes data. Today's humanists relentlessly teach this generation that the mind is the final authority on truth, that if something can't be rationalized and explained by the mind then it simply cannot be. There is no room allowed for the *super*-natural.

I'm here to encourage you today that God has been, is, and always will be "exceedingly abundantly" beyond our thinking (Ephesians 3:20). Without believing that He is, it is impossible to please Him.

We must learn how to be vessels that are yielded to the Holy Spirit, and allow God to work His lessons into us as we travel on this faith adventure. Many times God does something in me which then takes me days, weeks or months to process.

This is how I view praying "in the Spirit," or speaking in tongues: it is the supernatural activity of opening yourself up to God's Spirit flowing through you.

What Does the Bible Say?

The Bible addresses several different aspects of praying in tongues:

1. Tongues and their interpretation (1 Corinthians 14, especially vss. 5, 27-28);
2. Different dialects of tongues (Acts 2:7-11); and
3. Tongues as a private communion language (1 Corinthians 14: 4,14).

Tongues and their interpretation. 1 Corinthians teaches that when the Holy Spirit moves on a person in a public setting like a church and that person speaks in a language unknown to him, then it is desirable if someone there is gifted with the interpretation of tongues so that the utterances move from a personal stirring to understandable words that edify the congregation.

Different dialects of tongues. As the Spirit moves certain people can speak in a different known dialect. That's what happened in Acts 2:7-11. The believers secreted away in the house began to speak freely in different languages – eighteen of them are listed – that all hailed "the wonderful works of God" (v.11). When people led by the Spirit speak in a different dialect of tongues, people should hear words about God and His wonderful works.

Tongues as a private language of communion. This will be my focus for the rest of this chapter. I believe it will have a great impact on your personal prayer life.

> **Tongues take you "heavenly," into the place of meditation, awe and wonder... where we can be still and know that God is God.**

The Apostle Paul says we must develop praying with our understanding and also praying in the Spirit. He says, "I thank my God I speak with tongues more than you all...." (1 Corinthians 14:18). It is neither one nor the other, but both. Why has our praying, at least in America, become so lop-sided toward praying with our understanding? Is it the soiled footprints of our earthbound "mind culture" that we track across God's holy and supernatural ground?

One thing is clear: the devil wants us locked into earthly, sensual, demonic things. He doesn't want us to "go heavenly." Tongues take us "heavenly," into the place of meditation, awe and wonder. Praying in tongues takes us to a place where we can be still and know that

God is God (Psalm 40:10). Never lose your wonder!

We must set aside times to pray in tongues before God in our secret place. As we develop this type of prayer, rivers of living water begin to flow in us and out through us to the world (John 7:37-39). It is a discipline and it is an exercise.

When we are so at a loss we don't even know how to pray about something, that is when we're invited to turn to the Spirit and pray in tongues. Romans 8:26 teaches us that the Spirit will take hold together with us and bring the will of God to pass concerning that vexing situation.

When we pray in the Spirit we supercharge our inner man (1 Corinthians 14:4). In Jude 20 we read, "But you, beloved, building yourselves up on your most holy faith, praying in the Holy Spirit...." This word for "building" in the Greek derives from the root word *oikodomeo* which means "to build, to be a builder, to finish a building." When you pray in the Spirit you are building onto your spiritual house.

When you pray in the Spirit your joy comes back! Your peace comes back! Pastor, your first love revives! Affirmations come to us from the Spirit that we are indeed the beloved children of a mighty God (Romans 8:16).

There are times when I'm perplexed about a situation at home or in my ministry. I go to my secret place and pray in tongues. As I do this, God blesses me with wisdom and insight into the situation. He shows me what to do next.

Don't limit your praying in tongues to your morning time with God. Pray in tongues when you walk, drive, exercise, work, eat, play. Pray in tongues while lying in bed. Pray without ceasing (1 Thessalonians 5:17)! I will sometimes sing a simple song, like "Alleluia, alleluia!" in English and then just shift into tongues. As Paul says, "I will sing with the spirit" (1 Corinthians 14:15), so free yourself to "let it rip," singing in tongues. When I do this, God's presence never fails to fill me and my situation.

As I wait in His presence He gives me ears to hear His instructions. Hearing is the next step after listening. Hearing and listening can be many miles apart, as you know. As I still my soul God is able to be God. As I lift up my eyes and see God, I see how big and mighty He is. As I see His will and word for my situation I invite the King of Glory to come in and take over (Psalm 24:7). I open up and allow His Holy Spirit to flow through me.

We will make progress in our spiritual lives as we pray in other tongues and build with the Holy Spirit. This is how we keep ourselves in the love and compassion of Christ (Jude 21). This is how we finish strong! Yield yourself to the Holy Spirit in tongues, my friend, and let the river of life flow into you and out through you to water the nations.

Baptized in the Holy Spirit?

When we receive the gift of speaking in tongues that we do not understand the Bible says we're baptized in the Holy Spirit. When we are baptized in the Holy Spirit the Holy Spirit is not just resident, He becomes our President. If you are not baptized in the Holy Spirit this section and the following Scriptures are for you!

You can be born again and going to heaven, but not be baptized in the Spirit, and that's fine, it is miraculous nonetheless. But I am hungry! I want more! I want every single thing God has waiting for me! Do you feel the same way I do?

It all starts with desire (1 Corinthians 14:1). Desire spiritual things. Desire to receive the gift of tongues. Ask your Father to give you the fullness of His Holy Spirit and He will (Luke 11:13).

Have other Spirit-filled people pray with you to receive. As you pray, asking your Abba for the good gift of tongues, meditate on the Scriptures on the following pages. Ask God to fill you with His presence. Believe and receive.

Yield yourself to the Holy Spirit in tongues, my friend, and let the river of life flow into you and out through you to water the nations.

And get ready because this is the power of God that will fill you and make you an effective tool in His hands (Acts 1:8). Every person I know who is impacting the world is flowing in the baptism of the Holy Spirit.

Scriptures on Receiving the Baptism of the Holy Spirit

As you are seeking God for the baptism of the Holy Spirit, I offer the following Scriptures for you to chew on. As Peter makes clear in Acts 2:39, the promise of the Holy Spirit is for you, your children and for all those who are far off.

Behold, I send the Promise of My Father upon you; but tarry in the city of Jerusalem until you are endued with power from on high.

LUKE 24:49

If you then, being evil, know how to give good gifts to your children, how much more will your heavenly Father give the Holy Spirit to those who ask Him!

LUKE 11:13

And do not be drunk with wine, in which is dissipation; but be filled with the Spirit....

EPHESIANS 5:18

...he said to them, "Did you receive the Holy Spirit when you believed?"

ACTS 19:2A

But you shall receive power when the Holy Spirit has come upon you; and you shall be witnesses to Me in Jerusalem, and in all Judea and Samaria, and to the end of the earth.

ACTS 1:8

And they were all filled with the Holy Spirit and began to speak with other tongues, as the Spirit gave them utterance.

ACTS 2:4

For the promise is to you and to your children, and to all who are afar off, as many as the Lord our God will call.

Acts 2:39

But you, beloved, building yourself up in the most holy faith, praying in the Holy Spirit....

Jude 20

He who speaks in a tongue edifies himself, but he who prophesies edifies the church.

1 Corinthians 14:4

For if I pray in a tongue, my spirit prays, but my understanding is unfruitful.

1 Corinthians 14:14

May we desire communion with the Holy Spirit not just on Sundays but seven days a week. As we commune with Him we will live a fulfilled life in Christ and receive everything we need to walk out God's destiny for us.

Truly, the key is in the closet.